STILL PROTESTING

STILL PROTESTING
Why the Reformation Matters

D. G. Hart

Reformation Heritage Books
Grand Rapids, Michigan

Still Protesting
© 2018 by D. G. Hart

Reformation Heritage Books
2965 Leonard St. NE
Grand Rapids, MI 49525
616–977–0889
orders@heritagebooks.org
www.heritagebooks.org

Printed in the United States of America
18 19 20 21 22 23/10 9 8 7 6 5 4 3 2 1

Library of Congress Cataloging-in-Publication Data

Names: Hart, D. G. (Darryl G.), author.
Title: Still protesting : why the Reformation matters / D.G. Hart.
Description: Grand Rapids, Michigan : Reformation Heritage Books, 2018.
    Includes bibliographical references and index.
Identifiers: LCCN 2018014538 (print) | LCCN 2018021547 (ebook) | ISBN
    9781601786036 (epub) | ISBN 9781601786029 (pbk. : alk. paper)
Subjects: LCSH: Reformation.
Classification: LCC BR305.3 (ebook) | LCC BR305.3 .H37 2018 (print) |
    DDC 270.6—dc23
LC record available at https://lccn.loc.gov/2018014538

For additional Reformed literature, request a free book list from Reformation Heritage Books at the above regular or e-mail address.

To Everett Henes

CONTENTS

FOREWORD

I first saw it coming back in 1979. A year after he was elected pope, John Paul II paid his first visit to the United States, which included an outdoor Mass in Boston Common. Shortly afterward I spoke with a seminary classmate who attended, and he gushed, "It was the most intense spiritual experience of my life." Detecting, perhaps, a note of skepticism in my countenance, he quickly added, "And keep in mind, I've been to two Urbana Conferences!" The reference was not lost on me. Before there were Together for the Gospel or Ligonier Conferences, there were the triennial Urbana Conferences of InterVarsity Christian Fellowship, where evangelical luminaries encouraged upward of twenty thousand students to consider dedicating their lives to international missions. This new pope was bigger than Urbana? Wow.

I've lost touch with that classmate, and I don't know whether he eventually "poped," but he was by no means the only evangelical to have been bedazzled by the twenty-eight-year-long magisterium. Soon afterward, some evangelicals began to refer to the pope as J2P2—so now he ranked with *Star Wars*? Eventually the pope's winsomeness prompted likeness to the greatest of evangelical icons: "Many of the things said of the pope you'd say of Billy Graham," Timothy George observed.

Darryl Hart understands why Rome is popular, and *Still Protesting* is a long overdue response to the temptation to view it that way. Hart takes on the common arguments: Protestantism has a beauty deficit (our churches are drab); an intellectual deficit (Roman

Catholics seem smarter); and a unity deficit (Rome is one church—
or so it seems). In these and in other respects, much of Protestantism has lost its way. Moreover, Hart explains how the standard
Protestant polemics against Rome often do not hold sway in a post-
Christian America.

While acknowledging the malaise of Protestantism, Hart exposes
the reality behind the glitz of Rome. It is as prone to corruption in
modern times as it was during the Reformation, and there is profound
disunity and ongoing theological confusion within its ranks (persis-
tent interpretive pluralism is not a uniquely Protestant concern).

But this book offers more than a better anti-Roman Catholicism,
as timely as that is. Hart reminds readers of the enduring strengths
of historic Protestantism, distinguishing it from contemporary
counterfeit expressions in mainline or evangelical forms. Historic
Protestantism is grounded in the Reformation confessions, and Hart
lets those confessions do much of the talking, citing sources from
the Ten Theses of Berne to the Westminster Standards. From a confessional perspective, recent ecumenical overtures from Rome are
less than encouraging signs. The basis of those discussions is doctrinal indifference, and we should remember what that yielded a
century ago.

Still Protesting provides insight into the appeal of modern Roman
Catholicism. But it also explains why the Roman Catholic Church is
still a dangerous place for souls to reside.

John Muether
Professor of Church History and Dean of Libraries
Reformed Theological Seminary, Orlando

PREFACE

This book is a defense of Reformed Protestantism in opposition to some of the leading claims made by popular defenders of Roman Catholicism, many of whom are converts from Protestantism. For some readers, such a Protestant polemic against Roman Catholicism might look like another example of anti-Catholicism. For instance, the religious historian Mark Massa argues in *Anti-Catholicism in America: The Last Acceptable Prejudice* (2003) that Roman Catholics and Protestants see the world in inherently different ways, and this divergence leads to frequent misrepresentations of Roman Catholicism at almost every level of American society, from politics to Hollywood. Philip Jenkins, another historian, made a similar argument in *The New Anti-Catholicism: The Last Acceptable Prejudice* (2003) and claimed that prejudice against Roman Catholics in the United States is so deeply ingrained that for many it is invisible. These arguments lead to this question: Is *Still Protesting* another instance of America's "last acceptable prejudice"?

One way to respond is to notice the difference between illegitimate prejudice and theological conviction. In 1844, when Protestants in Philadelphia marched to protest the disloyalty of Roman Catholics to the United States (discussed in chapter 9), they exhibited a bigotry based on a political outlook that assumed someone loyal to the pope could not be a good American citizen. The same was true of Paul Blanshard's attack on Roman Catholics almost a century later in his best-selling book *American Freedom and Catholic Power* (1949), which instructed Americans that Roman Catholic understandings of church hierarchy, tradition, and loyalty were fundamentally at odds with national political ideals of liberty and democracy.

For the last fifteen years I have lived and worked with enough Roman Catholics to know that those objections are not simply prejudicial but wrong. In fact, I have enjoyed Roman Catholic colleagues sometimes even more than evangelical peers because the former do not suffer from a kind of piety that sometimes may reduce Christianity to an earnest relationship with Jesus. Because of a long tradition of intellectual reflection about most aspects of the human condition, Roman Catholics have been some of the most pleasant interlocutors, dinner companions, and departmental colleagues. Even if we wind up disagreeing about a movie, a politician, or a text in the curriculum, I invariably come away from a conversation wiser than before. Furthermore, even if the Vatican's politics may force Roman Catholics in the United States into awkward political stances, their loyalty to the magisterium is not much more bizarre than an average American Protestant's fascination with Britain's royal family.

Nevertheless, politics and culture are one thing, doctrine and worship another. In 2008, when Mark Noll and Carolyn Nystrom wrote their provocatively titled book *Is the Reformation Over? An Evangelical Assessment of Contemporary Roman Catholicism*, they took note of a number of arenas in which Protestants and Roman Catholics had found common cause, especially in contested political subjects surrounding procreation and marriage. They also observed some doctrinal developments among Roman Catholics that seemed to remove historic Protestant objections to Rome. These apparent changes—Rome's defenders are always averse to using the word "change" to describe the current stance of the church—accompanied Protestant fatigue with the sort of doctrinal rigidity typical supposedly of fundamentalist sectarianism.

Whatever readers may make of current trends among Roman Catholics and Protestants, the debates that divided the two sides of Western Christianity still matter. At least that is the contention of this book. If someone cares about the holiness of God, the demands of His law, human sinfulness, and the reality of eternal punishment for disobeying Him, the teachings that Protestants and Roman Catholics give to those questions are among the weightiest matters of human existence. Because Protestants at the Reformation (and many still do) argued that Rome's teaching on salvation was leading people astray, good reasons exist for opposing Roman Catholicism.

Of course this book addresses one side of the debate that has divided Protestants and Roman Catholics and considers only a part of the many reasons that prompted the Reformation and the Counter-Reformation. It emerges particularly from the context of the increasing number of Protestants who convert to Roman Catholicism, and its aim is to address some of the most frequent reasons given for abandoning Protestantism. Many of the explanations for conversion discuss the cultural crisis of the West, the beauty of Rome's architecture and liturgy, the comprehensiveness of Roman Catholicism's teaching, the history of Christianity in Europe, and the appeal of a social order that Christendom embodied. These aspects of Roman Catholicism can at times be impressive—but the Polka Mass that came with post-Vatican II liturgical freedom, not so much. When it comes to the saving work of Christ, worshiping God in a way that honors and glorifies Him, and maintaining pressure on church officers to be faithful in their oversight of God's people, however, the appeal of art, social teaching, or philosophy fades—that is, if salvation, worship, and the Christian ministry are more important than politics and culture. If salvation, worship, and the institutional church still matter, so does the Protestant Reformation.

Thanks go to colleagues at Hillsdale College, Matthew Gaetano and Korey Maas, who read parts of this book and provided helpful comments. It is dedicated to Everett Henes, pastor at Hillsdale Orthodox Presbyterian Church (Michigan), who has tried for the better part of a decade to nurture a congregation that is Reformed according to the Word of God.

INTRODUCTION:
ARE PROTESTANTS LOSING?

"Winning!" is an expression that Christians generally should not use to describe their church or denomination's accomplishments, but observers could use it to describe the rivalry between Protestantism and Roman Catholicism. Though Christian Smith, an accomplished sociologist of religion at the University of Notre Dame, does not use the word explicitly, his book *How to Go from Being a Good Evangelical to a Committed Catholic in Ninety-Five Difficult Steps* gives the distinct impression of Rome's victory over Protestants. Nowhere is this advantage more evident, according to Smith, than in the world of ideas. At one point, he gives an impressive list of Roman Catholic intellectuals, including Russell Kirk, Karol Wojtyla, G. K. Chesterton, J. R. R. Tolkien, Walker Percy, Flannery O'Connor, Mary Ann Glendon, William F. Buckley Jr., and Robert P. George. Smith concludes his who's who of Christian intellectuals this way: "And, for that matter, what's up with the fact that six of the nine Supreme Court justices (at the time of this writing) are Catholic, while there has never been one modern evangelical serving on the Court?"[1]

One of the intellectuals Smith omits is a man who would have been one of the early members of the United States Supreme Court's team of Roman Catholic justices—Robert Bork. At the time of his controversial nomination in 1987, Bork was actually a Protestant, though not one of strong conviction. As he explained in an interview

---

1. Christian Smith, *How to Go from Being a Good Evangelical to a Committed Catholic in Ninety-Five Difficult Steps* (Eugene, Ore.: Cascade Books, 2011), 78.

with the *National Catholic Register:* "Until age 12, I was going to a United Presbyterian Church. My mother and father belonged to two different Presbyterian denominations. Our faith wasn't terribly important growing up. My mother was interested in spiritual matters, but she was somewhat eclectic about it." But in 2003, at the age of seventy-six, Bork converted to the Roman Catholic Church. His reason involved partly the belief that this was the "Church that Christ established." He added that "while it's always in trouble, despite its modern troubles it has stayed more orthodox than almost any church I know of. The mainline Protestant churches are having much more difficulty."[2]

Mainline or evangelical Protestant conversions to Rome were not unimaginable when Ronald Reagan, the president who nominated Bork for the Supreme Court, began his tenure. But in 1980, Reformed Protestantism appeared to be the place where smart Christians in the United States put their intellectual capital. At the popular level, Francis Schaeffer, who had supplied tools for Christian reflection about philosophy and the arts to evangelical baby boomers, was gaining a whole new audience by convincing the emerging leaders of the religious right about the importance of worldview thinking. At the same time, a renaissance of Christian scholarship was emerging among academics who labored, for the most part, in Reformed Protestant vineyards. George Marsden and Mark Noll in history and Nicholas Wolterstorff and Alvin Plantinga in philosophy were establishing themselves as prominent figures in their respective fields while at the same time writing for *The Reformed Journal*, a high-word-count, no-graphics magazine that any Protestant academic with an ounce of intellectual playfulness read. This was the era also when James Montgomery Boice, John Gerstner, and R. C. Sproul impressed church members and pastors with their presentations at the Philadelphia Conference on Reformed Theology on the doctrines of grace as

---

2. Tim Drake, "Catholic Convert Judge Robert Bork Dies," *National Catholic Register Blogs, National Catholic Register*, December 19, 2012, http://www.ncregister.com/blog/tim-drake/catholic-convert-judge-robert-bork-dies#ixzz2H0XMixZ6.

understood and defended by Calvinists. In 1980, for aspiring scholars (like the author) and for evangelicals who longed for a faith with
intellectual substance, Reformed Protestantism appeared to be the
best—if not the only—game in American Protestantism.

That was also about the same time that the Vatican's College of
Cardinals elected John Paul II to be pope, an office he would hold
until 2005, making him the pontiff with the second-longest reign
in Roman Catholic history. His popularity was almost immediate,
as his 1980 tour of the United States proved, but his philosophical
and theological reflections would take awhile to turn heads. Help-
ing John Paul II gain the attention of American Protestants was his
Polish background and opposition to Communism. At a time when
the American political left and right differed dramatically over U.S.-
Soviet relations, Protestants in this country began to notice Rome's
history of resistance to Communism when Polish workers in Soli-
darity, an independent labor union, challenged Soviet hegemony and
received the pope's blessing. For political conservatives of Protestant background, having the Vatican on your side was just one more
indication of how bad Communism was. After the fall of the Berlin
Wall in 1989, an event for which Pope John Paul II received much
credit, he continued to impress American Protestants with thought-
ful encyclicals on capitalism, sexual reproduction, and human nature.
By the mid-1990s, in a race for the mind of American Christianity,
Roman Catholicism was running even with—if not ahead of—
Reformed Protestantism among evangelical Protestants in the United
States. An important indication of this new dynamic was Evangelicals
and Catholics Together, a statement produced by a group of Roman
Catholic and Protestant conservatives led by Richard John Neuhaus
and Chuck Colson, which explored the length and depth of a united
Christian front in the culture wars of the United States in particular
and the West more generally.

These dynamics explain in part the decision of an evangelical
scholar like Christian Smith to join the Roman Catholic Church.
In *How to Go from Being a Good Evangelical to a Committed Catholic in Ninety-Five Difficult Steps*, Smith tallies up the anomalies of

evangelical Protestantism and the strengths of Roman Catholicism to conclude that Rome's account of Christianity makes better sense not only of "reality" but also of Protestantism's defects. Once an evangelical recognizes these anomalies, he experiences an "aha" moment in which he realizes that "the Catholic paradigm simply works better—all things considered—than the evangelical paradigm."[3] For Smith, moving from Protestantism to Rome is akin to the way scientific discoveries take place. Scholars discover new data that older scientific models cannot explain and so look for a new paradigm. He concedes that some Protestants convert to Rome for aesthetic reasons or as part of a mystical, intuitive experience. But for Smith, an academic reared in evangelicalism, an intellectual model of conversion is just as plausible. Becoming a Roman Catholic, for Smith, means "a basic reorientation of assumptions, perceptions, and concerns that changes the way one views and lives life."[4] The impression he gives is that becoming Roman Catholic is a process and decision that involve being smarter than remaining Protestant.

The recognition of Rome's intellectual appeal is also partly responsible for the question that Mark A. Noll and Carolyn Nystrom asked in their controversial 2008 book *Is the Reformation Over? An Evangelical Assessment of Contemporary Roman Catholicism*. The authors' answer is maybe. Their question follows from important changes within both evangelical Protestantism and Roman Catholicism. Born-again Protestants have engaged in significant self-criticism. They have observed shortcomings in "ecclesiology, tradition, the intellectual life, sacraments, theology of culture, aesthetics, philosophical theology, [and] historical consciousness."[5] Meanwhile, Rome has changed from a hostile and forbidding communion to one that is open to dialogue and curious about those outside the Roman Catholic fold. Ironically, this shift, as David Wells observed almost fifty years ago

---

3. Smith, *How to Go*, 150.

4. Smith, *How to Go*, 5.

5. Mark A. Noll and Carolyn Nystrom, *Is the Reformation Over?: An Evangelical Assessment of Contemporary Roman Catholicism* (Grand Rapids: Baker Academic, 2008), 70.

about the immediate repercussions of the Second Vatican Council (also known as Vatican II), likely signaled that Rome was becoming increasingly open to "the influences of theological liberalism."[6] This is ironic because many of the evangelical Protestants who do convert to Rome do so precisely because they believe it provides intellectual and theological ballast to doctrinal equivocation and ecclesiastical disorganization. In a piece that Scott McKnight wrote about evangelical converts to Rome, their dominant reason was intellectual certainty. These Protestants joined the Roman Catholic Church "to transcend the limits of knowledge to find certainty," "to transcend the human limits of temporality to find connection to the entire history of the Church," and "to transcend the human limits of interpretive diversity to find an interpretive authority."[7] (This book will question whether any ecclesiastical institution, even one with the strictest construction of papal infallibility—a position qualified at Vatican II—can transcend human limits.)

The one area where Roman Catholicism did clearly offer clarity and certainty, as Richard John Neuhaus, founding editor of *First Things* as well as architect of Evangelicals and Catholics Together, explained, was morality. In 1990, when he entered the Roman Catholic Church, the largest Lutheran communion in the United States, the Evangelical Lutheran Church of America (ELCA), like many mainline Protestant denominations, was in the process of revising biblical teaching on homosexuality and marriage. This was an important factor for Neuhaus, a former ELCA minister, who recognized Rome's moral authority since the Roman Catholic Church still held the line on a host of issues related to sex and gender—abortion, contraception, adultery, divorce, and homosexuality. What Neuhaus disregarded was that the Lutheran Church–Missouri Synod, which he had left during the 1970s inerrancy controversies, was also holding the line against sexual license. For some reason, the conservatism of confessional Protestantism was less appealing and noteworthy than

---

6. Noll and Nystrom, *Is the Reformation Over?*, 60.
7. Scott McKnight, quoted in Noll and Nystrom, *Is the Reformation Over?*, 72.

the morality of one of the world's oldest religious institutions, the Vatican, which also happened to have sumptuous offices in some of the world's largest and oldest cities compared to the Missouri Synod's modest facilities in St. Louis.

But Neuhaus's reasons for converting were not simply that Protestants in the West were becoming feckless while Rome offered moral and intellectual certainty. He also echoed the sort of nonchalance suggested by Smith, Noll, and Nystrom—namely, that differences between Roman Catholics and Protestants were not nearly as grave as in the sixteenth century and that continuities were more apparent than not. Neuhaus explained that he grew up with all sorts of reasons for not thinking the divisions between Rome and Lutheranism were great, but "the Lutheran chapter in the history of the Church did occasion schism." While blame extended to both sides of the Reformation, "the division was tragic but not necessary."[8] In fact, the main difference between Protestantism and Roman Catholicism for Neuhaus was that Rome offered more of what Protestants already believed and practiced. Rome especially had the means to protect the faith—namely, the church. According to Neuhaus, "From my boyhood intuitions as an ecclesial Christian, it seemed self-evident that, if God intended to reveal any definite truths for the benefit of humankind, and if Jesus intended a continuing community of discipleship, then some reliable means would be provided for the preservation and transmission of such truths through the centuries." Rome's heritage of the apostles and their successors, the bishops, ensures authority and the perseverance of the Christian witness. Neuhaus quoted Avery Cardinal Dulles to explain the infallibility of the popes and magisterium as "another way of saying that the Holy Spirit will preserve the Church against using its full authority to require its members to assent to what is false." Unlike many former evangelicals' conversions, influenced by the intellectual appeal of Rome, Neuhaus's conversion

---

8. Richard John Neuhaus, "How I Became the Catholic I Was," *First Things*, April 2002, https://www.firstthings.com/article/2002/04/how-i-became-the-catholic-i-was.

was more institutional. But it was nonetheless a clear indication that Protestantism could not measure up to Rome's superior claims.

As plausible and as well intended as are some of the reasons that many former Protestants have given lately for joining the Roman Catholic Church, they are not sufficient to overcome the enormous problems in Roman Catholicism that the Reformation exposed. To be sure, Protestantism's critics are correct to charge that the churches that have descended from the Reformers have lost their way. Mainline Protestantism, once a formidable presence in American life, is a shell of its former self and is increasingly absorbed with an egalitarian understanding of Christianity that welcomes diversity in all forms (demographic, theological, and moral), except for those believers who insist the church should not turn a blind eye to personal sin or doctrinal error. Although they still affirm Christianity's supernatural character (as opposed to Protestant liberalism's abandonment of it), evangelical Protestants represent a smorgasbord of doctrinal emphases, worship styles, and ecclesiastical and parachurch ministries that nurtures incoherence as much as it relies on earnestness. According to Noll and Nystrom, evangelicalism is weak in "ecclesiology, tradition, the intellectual life, sacraments, theology of culture, aesthetics, philosophical theology, [and] historical consciousness."[9] Smith is blunter and concludes that evangelicalism has "many serious problems" that Roman Catholicism "solves."[10] Given contemporary American Protestantism's state of affairs, Rome's hierarchy, institutional comprehensiveness, intellectual resources, and relative moral clarity (can the converts really overlook the scandals of sexually abusive priests and the hierarchy's cover-up?) look much more appealing and seem to be a more reliable expression of Christianity than Protestantism. Not to be missed is that since Vatican II, Roman Catholicism is now much friendlier than it once appeared when its curia looked too ornate for Low-Church Protestant sensibilities and its dogmatic utterances about "no salvation outside the church" seemed too narrow

---

9. Noll and Nystrom, *Is the Reformation Over?*, 71.
10. Smith, *How to Go*, 172.

for evangelicalism's capacity to evangelize everywhere and at all times through any means available. Evangelicals, according to Noll and Nystrom, "find among Catholics, besides a lot of dross, a functioning concept of church, a powerful Christian sense of the material world, and a long tradition of balanced political theology."[11] That dross is an aspect of Rome's existence that converts like Smith conveniently overlook. Ironically, Rome's anomalies post–Vatican II undermine the reasons for conversion since going from evangelicalism to Roman Catholicism is to exchange one set of problems for another.

This book, however, is not about Rome's contemporary difficulties as much as it is about the real and abiding strengths of the Protestant Reformation as a critique of the Western church five centuries ago. Despite dramatic changes within the ecclesiastical landscape over the last fifty years, the status of human beings before a holy and righteous God and the message of the gospel as explained by the Reformers remain the same. Indeed, the great truths of the Protestant Reformation are still as poignant and compelling as they were in the sixteenth century—truth is, after all, supposed to be timeless. Martin Luther, arguably the pithiest exponent of Protestantism and critic of Western Christianity at the time of the Reformation, wrote in his treatise "On the Freedom of a Christian" (1520):

> Here we must point out that the entire Scripture of God is divided into two parts: commandments and promises. Although the commandments teach things that are good, the things taught are not done as soon as they are taught, for the commandments show us what we ought to do but do not give us the power to do it. They are intended to teach man to know himself, that through them he may recognize his inability to do good and may despair of his own ability.... Therefore, in order not to covet and to fulfil the commandment, a man is compelled to despair of himself, to seek the help which he does not find in himself elsewhere and from someone else, as stated in Hosea [13:9]: "Destruction is your own, O Israel: your help is only in me." As we fare with respect to one commandment, so we fare

---

11. Noll and Nystrom, *Is the Reformation Over?*, 249.

with all, for it is equally impossible for us to keep any one of them. Now when a man has learned through the commandments to recognize his helplessness and is distressed about how he might satisfy the law—since the law must be fulfilled so that not a jot or tittle shall be lost, otherwise man will be condemned without hope—then, being truly humbled and reduced to nothing in his own eyes, he finds in himself nothing whereby he may be justified and saved.

Thus far Luther has given a description of a person's plight when confronted by God's holy character and law. But, as Luther also explained when turning to Scripture's promises, God does not leave men and women and boys and girls in this fearful state:

Here the second part of Scripture comes to our aid, namely, the promises of God which declare the glory of God, saying, "If you wish to fulfil the law and not covet, as the law demands, come, believe in Christ in whom grace, righteousness, peace, liberty, and all things are promised you. If you believe, you shall have all things; if you do not believe, you shall lack all things." That which is impossible for you to accomplish by trying to fulfil all the works of the law—many and useless as they all are—you will accomplish quickly and easily through faith. God our Father has made all things depend on faith so that whoever has faith will have everything, and whoever does not have faith will have nothing.[12]

That may sound too good to be true. Indeed, the history of Christianity is littered with professing believers, from the Judaizers and monks to Wesleyans and theonomists, who added demands and duties to the free offer of the gospel, designed supposedly with good intentions to prevent Christians from being so passive and dependent in salvation. By doing more, believers might prove their personal holiness and

---

12. Martin Luther, "On the Freedom of a Christian," in *First Principles of the Reformation*, ed. Henry Wace and C. A. Buchheim (London: John Murray, 1883; Fordham University Modern History Sourcebook), https://sourcebooks.fordham.edu/mod/luther-freedomchristian.asp.

show themselves worthy. But it was the genius of the Reformation to tell sinners that their only hope for a perfect, sinless life was to trust in Christ and by faith receive their Savior's perfect righteousness as their own. Only on that basis could a sinner bear to stand before a holy and righteous God on judgment day.

It was also the accomplishment of Protestantism to assert these truths in the context of a church that had grown fat and lazy. The Renaissance papacy was occupied with rebuilding Rome as a center for pilgrims to venerate relics and with asserting its power within European politics. Practically everyone in Western Europe believed that Rome needed reform. Humanists, monks, priests, nuns, and even bishops knew that the papacy had become corrupt and was abusing its privileges. Protestants were the only ones, though, to carry out a program of reform. That plan included revising a theology of salvation that increased the holdings in Rome's coffers (paying for indulgences) and sometimes kept civil authorities in submission to the alleged Vicar of Christ. Reform also included changes in worship that took away the veneration of saints and returned Christ, as the sole mediator between God and man, to the center of devotion; His righteousness alone could satisfy God's just demands, and His work makes purgatory senseless. Protestants also proposed a variety of ways to reform church government. Presbyterians may have been the most systematic by creating a system that built checks and balances into church government so that the tyranny that so often afflicts rule by one (monarchy or papacy) might be prevented. Protestants did not merely tinker with Rome's way of being the church. The Reformers overhauled Roman Catholicism because it was corrupt and obscured the good news of Christ's salvation.

And yet Protestantism's reformation program was one that Rome rejected and even condemned at the Council of Trent (where efforts were made to forbid abuses)—one that Roman Catholics still refuse to accept even as the magisterium's teachings on salvation become murkier than those of the Counter-Reformation. The truths of the Reformation are also, sadly, in neglect among evangelical and mainline Protestants who, through a quest either for personal holiness or social justice, have lost sight of Luther's and Calvin's genius. Changes among Roman Catholics and evangelicals may suggest they have become closer to each other, but that growing proximity has more to do with forgetfulness and confusion about the claims of both Rome and Protestants at the time of the Reformation than it does with doctrinal or ecumenical breakthroughs. Some contend that the Reformation stemmed from a misunderstanding and that now we can see past the points that caused both sides of the sixteenth century to stumble. But this apparently simple historical assertion ignores the clear words of the Reformed and Lutheran churches and Trent. Fuzziness about doctrine, the church, Scripture, and worship is not a reason for conversion, nor is it a sufficient barrier to prevent conversions. Even so, the Reformers were not confused or unclear; nor was the Council of Trent, even if subsequent popes and councils have tried to soften Rome's sixteenth-century teachings. For that reason the Reformation is not over. It needs to be recovered as much by would-be Protestants as by Roman Catholics because it explains how sinners become right with God.

This book is an effort to reassert, explain, and defend the truths that originally provoked the Protestant Reformation. It attempts particularly to set the origins of Protestantism in the historical context of the fifteenth and sixteenth centuries and thereby explain why Martin Luther and others found the plan of salvation available through Rome to be so inadequate, how they responded by looking to Scripture, and what the response from the church's hierarchy was. The first part of the book features the most important aspects—the genius, as it were—of Protestantism and why it happened (chapter 1). The Reformers drew on the teachings of the apostles (from whom the bishops were supposed to have succeeded) from the pages of Scripture and restored the Bible to the chief standard of divine authority (chapter 2).The examination of what the apostles wrote as opposed to what the church had instituted led Protestants to posit the doctrine of justification by faith alone, which was another way of asserting the sufficiency of Christ and His righteousness, as opposed to grace-infused holiness of regular Christians or saints for salvation (chapter 3).

Debates with Rome in turn led to challenges to papal authority and an inspection of the form of church government that Christ instituted through the apostles and recorded in Scripture (chapter 4). The Protestant doctrine of salvation also involved a different understanding of the Christian life—the idea of vocation—which made it possible for those who trusted in Christ to serve Him as priests (priesthood of all believers) in their ordinary callings as mothers, bakers, shepherds, and princes (chapter 5).

The second half of the book examines and attempts to refute some of the chief objections to Protestantism by Roman Catholic apologists and those who have converted to Rome. To the claim that Rome is the church that Jesus founded, chapter 6 shows that Roman Catholic historians know better and that the city of Rome was relatively late to Christian communities and shared the spotlight with other ancient cities as the origin of Christianity's formal structure. To the claim that Protestantism destroyed church unity and cannot help but churn out further divisions, chapter 7 examines the origins of the 1054 schism between the Eastern and Western churches to suggest that Rome's claims of unity are hollow. To the claim that Protestantism inherently neglects the arts and beauty in church life, chapter 8 examines how improper is the effort to represent or capture God in physical representations, no matter how beautiful, and why Protestants are rightly suspicious of artistic or architectural attempts to bring God down to earth. To the charge that Protestants launched a modern world that resulted in untold materialism, relativism, and disorder, chapter 9 shows that Protestants also opposed many of the worst features of modernity and were some of the fiercest critics of Christian efforts to adapt Christianity to the modern world, as in the case of Protestant modernism. Finally, to the argument that Rome does not change but that Protestantism has become liberal, the last chapter examines the major features of the Second Vatican Council and how it turned the Roman Catholic Church from a fierce defender of tradition into a body that has tried to come alongside the modern world—in other words, Vatican II liberalized Roman Catholicism.

In sum, this book is a reminder that Protestants—at least some of them—still protest what Roman Catholicism did to the Christianity the apostles received and taught in Scripture. For evangelicals who have led common causes with Roman Catholics on many social and cultural matters and who may be tempted to think that the sixteenth-century division was either a mistake or no longer relevant, what follows may help them to remember what was at stake in the Reformation and that Rome is still in need of reform. For liberal or mainline Protestants, this book is a reminder that the Reformation was not a way to modernize Western Christianity but chiefly an attempt to clarify the gospel, institute proper worship, and ensure sound teaching and biblical worship through a good order (government) in the church. For conservative Protestants of a confessional type, the book should refresh memories of the major debates of the Reformation and give them ammunition when addressing Roman Catholic friends or other Protestants who may be tempted to convert. Indeed, the book has emerged from the author's constant befuddlement at Protestants who think Roman Catholicism is the better form of Christianity and so leave the Protestant fold. Ideally, this book could function as an argument to prevent Protestants from converting. But experience shows that once a person's head has been turned by the apparent history, the hierarchy, the intellectual tradition, and the conservatism of Rome, arguments for Protestants are usually ineffective and beside the point. Yet for those who know people considering converting to Rome, this book might at least help them understand the appeal of Roman Catholicism and also remind them of why becoming Roman Catholic is erroneous. It explains many of the truths and claims that converts need to overlook in order to join Rome.

For any Roman Catholic who picks up this book, it may come across as another expression of America's oldest acceptable prejudice—anti-Catholicism. The hope is that in the pages that follow such readers will find arguments that make Protestant prejudice plausible. That is, Roman Catholic readers might come away with a better understanding from the Protestant perspective of why the Reformation happened and why today some Protestants still protest Roman

Catholicism. The hope as well is to make the objections to Rome not political or cultural but religious and theological. For too long, anti-Catholicism in the United States trafficked in conspiratorial or paranoid conceptions of the Vatican, bishops, priests, and nuns and portrayed Roman Catholics as unfit members of American society. The politics of citizenship and American government are not the concern of this book, even though the author understands that Protestant political prejudice against Roman Catholics was often vicious, unreasonable, and even wicked. Recognizing the poor quality of political anti-Catholicism, however, is not an excuse for overlooking the serious theological, liturgical, and ecclesial fault lines that still divide Protestants and Roman Catholics. This book is a brief foray into those sensitive areas. The intent is not to offend. Still, given the poignancy of the matters involved—salvation, personal identity and meaning, family traditions, understandings of history and the world—the book cannot help but be objectionable on some level.

The desire in raising these issues is not to refight the Reformation. It is to remember what was at stake in the sixteenth century and why Protestantism, for all its faults and missteps, still matters. The Reformers addressed the most basic question that confronts all human beings: How can a sinner be right with and worship in good conscience a righteous God who demands sinless perfection? Protestants used to believe that this question, along with the kind of life that followed from answers to it, was at the heart of their disagreement with Rome. This book arises from the conviction that the answers the Reformers supplied to life's most important questions on the basis of their study of the Bible and theological reflection are as superior today as they were when they provided the grounds for Christians in the West to abandon the bishop of Rome.

1

WHY THE REFORMATION HAPPENED

Martin Luther was not looking for a fight. When the Reformation began, he was an Augustinian monk who happened to teach in a city, Wittenberg, where events providentially conspired to underscore the need for ecclesiastical reform and provided shelter for protests against Rome's corruption. Born in 1483, the son of a successful miner in Saxony, Luther dashed his father's hopes for a career in law and set out instead for a life of devotion. The circumstance that led to this change of career was a fierce thunderstorm in 1505 in which Luther, then a university student, promised St. Anne, the mother of the virgin Mary, to enter a monastery if he survived the elements. He not only escaped the storm but that same year entered the Augustinian order. Two years later, he took priestly orders. In 1511, two years shy of his thirtieth birthday, Luther received directions to teach at the newly established university in Wittenberg, endowed in 1502 by Frederick the Wise, the elector of Saxony. Wittenberg was the first university in Germany founded without the permission of the church. That autonomy should not suggest defiance since Frederick was a devoted Roman Catholic who had one of the largest collections of relics in the Holy Roman Empire. Still, the university was Frederick's crown jewel, and he became a fierce defender of its faculty.

In 1510, a year before his appointment at Wittenberg, Luther visited Rome and became aware of the decadence of both the city and the clergy, but not in a way that set him on the path of reform. The shock he experienced while visiting the Eternal City was typical of the cultural clash that accompanied most northern European visitors to Rome. Upon his return to Germany, Luther assumed his duties at the university, which involved an explicit requirement to teach the Bible on its own terms. His lectures on the Psalter (1514) and Romans (1515) planted seeds that sprouted into Protestant teaching on justification. Still, the church reforms of which Luther became the cause célèbre were only implicit in his teaching as a professor. The lines of conflict did not become apparent until ideas debated in lecture halls had consequences for believers in the parish.

Many theologians, university faculty, and humanists were keenly aware of the church's flawed, if not corrupt, administration. The Western Schism (1378–1417) was the result of the papacy's deep alliances to European politicians and failure to mind its spiritual duties. It was a period when rival papacies claimed succession to the bishop of Rome, one in the French city of Avignon and one in Rome. To resolve this crisis, one that saw European monarchs and princes take sides, the Council of Constance (1414–1418), the same body that condemned John Wycliffe and Jan Hus, elected a third pope who became the "true" occupant of Peter's chair. In fact, the council represented one of the chief outlets for church reformers in the two centuries before Protestantism emerged. To counteract both the personal and political deficiencies of popes, officials and faculty recommended conciliarism—oversight by a council of bishops—as a better way to administer the church's ministry than rule by an ecclesiastical monarch in Rome. With the exception of the Church of England, Protestants picked up on conciliarism as a model for church government. John Calvin's *Ecclesiastical Ordinances* (1541) was arguably an attempt to draw on the elements of conciliarism in the form of presbyterian church government, oversight by elders and pastors—that is, presbyters meeting in assemblies and synods. Even so, conciliarism was only one expression of the fears church leaders had about an ecclesiastical hierarchy that seemed to act more out of self-interest than pastoral concern. Girolamo Savonarola, prior of the Dominican monastery in Florence, became famous for his fiery condemnations of the papacy, particularly the wantonly immoral Pope Alexander VI (1492–1503). The reasons for Savonarola's proclamation of impending divine judgment were not hard to fathom. Eamon Duffy observes that Alexander was "the most notorious of all the Renaissance popes," who had "a succession of mistresses with whom he lived quite openly." Europeans may have looked the other way at such behavior in their kings and princes. In fact, as the prince of the Papal States, Alexander showed himself to be more politician than pastor. Duffy adds that Alexander "used his children's dynastic marriages to form alliances with a succession of princes" and arranged for large tracts of land to create political territories for his sons.[1] If pious souls had wanted the church to pay attention to spiritual matters, where were they to turn?

Luther's concerns about personal holiness were no different from those of a host of theologians and humanists who sought clear teaching and examples from the church's priests, bishops, and monks on the Christian life as one of repentance. Renaissance humanists, who sought a new curriculum based on ancient texts including the Bible in the original languages, also promoted the good life and the love of virtue. Reforms of monasteries, especially among the Dominicans and Franciscans, rekindled forms of introspective piety and pastoral practice that saw monks leading the laity in religious devotion in pockets of Europe. Some bishops also took up the challenge of holiness, notably Guillaume Briçonnet, who became bishop of Meaux (northeast of Paris) in 1516 and put humanism to work in his diocese by appointing biblical scholars, including Calvin's future colleague William Farel, and establishing programs of regular preaching. What made Luther's call for reform different from the many efforts to call the church back to its true purpose was the Reformer's unintended discovery that changing the church's course was not a simple process. Even to do so at the local level, as Luther attempted, was to start the proverbial pulling of strings in a quilt. Once started, the whole patchwork unravels.

Luther first started to pick at the church's system of indulgences, which in turn led to serious questions about Rome's theology of

---

1. Eamon Duffy, *Saints and Sinners: A History of the Popes* (New Haven, Conn.: Yale University Press, 1997), 146.

salvation, which then raised questions about the hierarchy of bishops and the supremacy of the pope in church government. Isolating one piece of the puzzle of Roman Catholicism was impossible as events transpired in Wittenberg. Indulgences were a local economic concern in Saxony since they transferred money from the territory to Rome, where proceeds helped to pay for St. Peter's Basilica. Luther tapped local resentment over Rome's exploitation when he questioned the premise that purchasing an indulgence brought peace between God and a sinner. In his Ninety-Five Theses, he insisted that repentance should characterize the entire Christian life. He also took a swing at the hierarchy: "Christians should be taught that, if the Pope knew the exactions of the preachers of indulgences, he would rather have the basilica of St. Peter reduced to ashes than built with the skin, flesh, and bones of his sheep."[2] That punch not only stung Pope Leo X but also the local archbishop of Mainz, Albert of Brandenburg, who represented the sort of power-grabbing typical among the careerism of princes and bishops. Albert not only refused to give up his other bishoprics when he became archbishop but was also eager to have access to the Holy Roman Emperor, Charles V, as imperial chancellor, a position that went along with overseeing the archdiocese of Mainz. Part of the deal that Albert had arranged to be archbishop was to support the program of indulgence sales in his territory and so gain Leo's approval. In other words, Luther's theological challenge threatened much more than doctrine; it included the authority and finances of the church, along with the rules of Europe's political establishment.

If the threats that Luther posed were not sufficiently great to elevate to public prominence an obscure monk at a new and perhaps undistinguished university, circumstances in Wittenberg added fuel to the fire. One was Frederick the Wise's desire to promote his university and the faculty who taught there. Although the elector of Saxony never fully understood Luther's difficulties with Rome's teaching on sin, grace, repentance, and purgatory, he was keen to protect the man

---

2. Martin Luther, quoted in Diarmaid MacCulloch, *The Reformation* (New York: Penguin, 2003), 117.

who was putting Wittenberg's university on the map. That political protection literally saved Luther from being another Wycliffe or Hus, a condemned heretic burned at the stake. The elector ran interference for Luther with church and imperial officials and provided a safe haven for the Reformer. Equally important but not something Luther planned was a publishing industry in Wittenberg that took off with the professor's tracts and treatises and so sent the arguments for reform throughout German-speaking territories and cities. The papacy and local church officials were not prepared for the publicity. They originally thought Luther's ideas were part of a local controversy that had no bearing on Rome's larger aims and concerns. At the same time, the condemnations that came down on Luther in 1521 only increased interest in his affairs and ideas and therefore generated a wider audience for the relatively accessible writings that Wittenberg's printers produced. In retrospect, Rome's officials might have looked back on the events between 1517 and 1521, the time when Protestantism first sprouted, as a perfect storm that no one could have stopped. From Luther's side, this was an unplanned reformation. No one could have seen Protestantism emerge in this way. Even more unthinkable was an idea that it might succeed.

The leading authorities in Christendom, the Holy Roman Emperor Charles V and Pope Leo X, gave different verdicts to Luther's ideas—he had not yet proposed a program beyond taking issue with church teaching and practice. In 1520 the pope condemned Luther as a heretic in the papal bull *Exsurge Domine*, which the university professor in turn burned when he received a copy—to much great fanfare in the city of Wittenberg. Charles V was not quick to condemn but gave the monk a chance to defend himself at a meeting of the empire's princes arranged by Frederick the Wise. At the Diet of Worms in April 1521, where Luther allegedly uttered the famous line, "Here I stand; I can do no other," Charles gave the dissenter a chance to recant his writings, which had grown prodigious thanks to the talents of printers and the market for pamphlets. Here was the point where Luther portrayed the debate as one between rival authorities—either the papacy or Scripture. With prince and bishop

so dependent on each other both for secular and ecclesiastical oper-
ations within Christendom, Luther had no authorities to which to
appeal other than God's Word. Even so, he also framed his objections
to indulgences and papal authority into a complaint that resonated
with the experience of many churchmen, nobles, and Christians—
namely, that the papacy had lost sight of its proper function in pursuit
of worldly accomplishments. Luther explained to the emperor that
if he recanted his words and arguments, "all I shall achieve is to add
strength to tyranny, and open not the windows but the doors to this
monstrous godlessness, for a wider and freer range than it has ever
dared before."[3] Charles disagreed with Luther and even condemned
him as a heretic but granted safe passage so the professor could return
home. On the way, Frederick arranged a friendly kidnapping that
took Luther to Wartburg and kept him in hiding for ten months.

From that time on, because of Frederick's determination to protect his Bible professor, the politics of the Holy Roman Empire gave
Protestantism a foothold. From 1521 until 1526, princes decided
whether the churches in their territories would follow the traditions
of Rome or begin to reform in ways that Luther promoted. Politicians
were, in fact, key to the temporal success of the Reformation—
without magistrates, no Magisterial Reformation. Lutheranism took
root in a number of imperial cities where local princes chose reform
over the status quo. Reformed Protestantism also owed its initial success to the politics of the empire. Indeed, those places where a version
of Protestantism distinct from Lutheranism took shape were imperial cities that had gained political independence from the emperor
during the fourteenth and fifteenth centuries, such as Basel, Bern,
Strasbourg, and Zurich.

Reformed Protestantism before Calvinism

One of the people present for Luther's debate at the Heidelberg disputation of 1518 was a member of the Dominican order of monks,
Martin Bucer. Like many in the church who hoped for reform, Bucer,

---

3. Martin Luther, quoted in MacCulloch, *The Reformation*, 127.

as a result of his encounter with Luther's ideas, set into motion plans for restoring the church to its chief function in the cure of souls. The Dominican would eventually become the head of church reforms in one of the former imperial cities, Strasbourg, which became a testing ground for John Calvin's early ministry during the period when he was at odds with city officials in Geneva. But before Bucer could try his hand at reform, Strasbourg's magistrates needed to see what reformation might look like. Here the work of Ulrich Zwingli in Zurich was decisive.

Born in 1484—a year younger than Luther—Zwingli was a native of Switzerland and took pride in the territories' hard-fought independence (1499) from the Holy Roman Empire. He trained for the priesthood and became acquainted with the new curriculum that humanists advocated. Erasmus's understanding of practical Christianity had a significant influence on Zwingli early in his career. After serving the small town of Glarus, in 1518 Zwingli became the priest at the Great Church (Grossmünster) in Zurich. He claimed not to be a disciple of Luther, but news of German church developments as well as Swiss frustration with papal foreign policy pushed Zwingli to challenge church tradition. A famous incident in 1522 in which Zurich citizens ate sausage on the first Sunday of Lent—Zwingli was present but did not eat—proved to be the tipping point. The priest defended the act of defying religious custom by arguing that the Bible commanded no such observance of the church calendar or requirements for fasting. Like Luther, Zwingli appealed to the one religious authority available to Christians outside the church hierarchy or its own interpretation of tradition—Scripture. Soon other characteristics of Protestantism, though no one called it that, emerged. Zwingli was married months after the sausage incident. Another pastor in the city, Leo Jud, called for the destruction of images in the churches based on the Ten Commandments, an appeal that also led Jud to insist that the Decalogue be renumbered.[4] These challenges to church tradition in 1524 prompted city officials in Zurich to ban images. A year later,

---

4. Reformed Protestants separated Rome's first commandment into the first and

after debates about the sacraments absorbed Zwingli and the city's other pastors, city council also prohibited the Mass. In Zurich the rudiments of a program for church reform, different from Luther's, took root, displaying the hallmark signs of conforming the church's ministry to Scripture's clear instruction.

At roughly the same time that Zurich was turning Protestant, Strasbourg, a prominent imperial city of economic and religious importance in the Alsace region, underwent a similar set of changes. The preacher responsible for persuading residents and magistrates was Matthias Zell, who in 1523 started preaching ideas inspired by Luther about sin, grace, and the afterlife. Zell's efforts attracted other Protestant preachers, the most prominent of whom was Martin Bucer, who in 1520, after leaving the Dominicans, became a private secretary to the German humanist and reformer Ulrich von Hutten. By 1529 Zell and Bucer had convinced Strasbourg's council to ban the Mass. Given the political situation in the Holy Roman Empire, Bucer played an active role in trying to mediate differences between Luther and Zwingli who, after the Marburg Colloquy of 1529, had become bitter foes over the nature of the Lord's Supper. Political survival demanded Protestant unity in the face of Roman Catholic military aggression. Bucer also steered Strasbourg and his colleagues away from the radicalism of the Anabaptists, who were responsible in a way for the Peasants Revolt of 1524 when some confused the spiritual freedom of the gospel with overturning the social hierarchy. But to do so, he made church discipline an important component of church reform. Reformed Protestants could not simply change the apparatus of church ministry. Bucer was convinced that they also needed to live lives of repentance and holiness. Using community-elected elders within congregations and establishing church courts for oversight of church members' moral lives were among Bucer's goals. This emphasis on church discipline also raised an important issue of contention—whether the church or the city council (state) should be

---

second commandments and combined Rome's ninth and tenth commandments into a single tenth commandment.

the first court of jurisdiction in overseeing the morality of residents and citizens. That question even extended to whether the magistrate or the church had the authority of excommunication.

Soon, other cities in the Swiss confederation were dismantling the accretion of religious customs and spiritual lethargy that had piled up because of the church hierarchy's mismanagement. That German-speaking pastors were leaders was no accident. In Berne, Berthold Haller, born in Aldingen, Germany, orchestrated revisions in the city's churches that followed the Bible as the sole guideline. In 1528, Berne's pastors wrote one of Reformed Protestantism's earliest creeds, the Ten Theses of Berne, which was used originally for a debate but emerged as a statement of faith. These theses appealed to Christ as head of the church who had revealed His will through Scripture, called for reforms of worship that eliminated the Mass and images, denied the doctrine of purgatory, and opened the door for clergy to marry. Six years later the Swiss city of Basel issued its own confession of faith (1534). The chief pastor who led Basel's reformation was John Oecolampadius, another minister from Germany who was a year older than Luther. By the 1530s, Reformed Protestants, especially in German-speaking territories, needed to distinguish themselves from Anabaptists, which explains Basel's chapter on the legitimacy of the civil magistrate and his use of the sword to execute justice. The creed also explains more fully differences between Rome and Protestants on the sufficiency of Christ's righteousness received by faith alone, with good works being not "the satisfaction for sins" but the "fruit of faith." Like the churches of Zurich and Berne, Basel's churches abolished the Mass and forbade the devotional use of images.

When in 1536 the city council of Geneva established an alliance with the Swiss Confederacy—with especially close ties to Berne—Reformed Protestantism emerged as a force beyond the German-speaking territories and became truly international. That year coincides both with the city's citizens' vote to embrace Protestantism and with John Calvin's arrival in the city as a pastor called by the city council to oversee church reform. Prior to Calvin's arrival, Swiss politics had factored significantly in Geneva's religious identity.

The city needed protection from larger cities, and Fribourg (Roman Catholic) and Berne (Reformed) were the chief rivals. Geneva's embrace of Protestantism settled political alliances. The council's turn to Calvin was another indication of Geneva's neediness since the French Protestant was himself a recent convert (roughly 1534, according to most estimates) to the doctrines of grace. Calvin was also precocious. Only a year after his conversion, he had written his first edition of the *Institutes of the Christian Religion* and sent the book to King Francis of France, Calvin's native country. Calvin's inexperience was partially responsible for the Geneva authorities' determination to relinquish their ties with him, and he departed in 1538 for Strasbourg, where he benefited from Martin Bucer's wisdom. Calvin had demanded more reforms of church life than Geneva's magistrates could afford to make, for both religious and political reasons. Bucer, who had tried to be a mediating influence among Protestants, was a welcome counterbalance to the young Calvin's zeal.

Although Calvin had been reluctant to go to Geneva in the first place, when the city's magistrates in 1541 called on him again to lead the church he was still reluctant; he hoped to be a writer. But without a capable pastor at the helm, the church in Geneva was adrift. In 1539, when the nearby bishop Jacob Sadoleto wrote to the Genevans to persuade them to return to the Roman Catholic fold, the city's officials went back to Calvin for help. His reply to Sadoleto's letter was a succinct summary of Reformed Protestant convictions at a still early stage—only twenty-two years after Luther's Ninety-Five Theses. The Roman episcopacy was corrupt and incapable of reforming itself, Calvin observed. The pope and bishops had failed to maintain true worship and a right understanding of salvation. Worse, all they could do when challenged by Protestants was accuse the dissenters of seeking personal gain. Calvin's letter of response was an eloquent lament about the state of the Western church at the hands of officials more interested in politics and material gain than the church's ministry of word and sacrament. Simply to assert, as Sadoleto argued, that the bishops were carrying on what the church had always done was to ignore what Scripture taught; it was also to show the necessity of adding tradition to Scripture because the Bible offered little support for Rome's ceremonies. What was true for worship was equally the case for salvation. Whether out of indolence or ignorance, Rome had obscured the work of Christ and the sufficiency of His saving work for sinners:

> As all mankind are, in the sight of God, lost sinners, we hold that Christ is their only righteousness, since, by his obedience, he has wiped off our transgressions; by his sacrifice, appeased the divine anger; by his blood, washed away our stains; by his cross, borne our curse; and by his death, made satisfaction for us. We maintain that in this way man is reconciled in Christ to God the Father, by no merit of his own, by no value of works, but by gratuitous mercy. When we embrace Christ by faith, and come, as it were, into communion with him, this we term, after the manner of Scripture, the righteousness of faith.[5]

Calvin's reply succeeded in keeping Geneva Protestant, and it also gained an invitation for him to return as the chief pastor among the city's Company. From 1541 on, Geneva emerged as a vital center of Reformed Protestantism. To be sure, Zurich and Basel, with their universities and gifted pastors, also exerted significant influence on the subsequent reformations that arose in France, England, the Netherlands, Heidelberg, Scotland, and even in Eastern Europe (Hungary, Poland, and Lithuania). But Geneva became a model for many Protestants, and outside German-speaking territories Calvinism had a greater influence on second- and third-generation Protestants than Lutheranism. Some of that owed to differences between Lutherans and the Reformed over the Lord's Supper and some to Calvin's genius, especially the presbyterian church government that he established on his return to Geneva. In his *Ecclesiastical Ordinances*, Calvin added the structural reforms that revisions of theology and worship needed to survive. Episcopacy had proven itself susceptible to corruption and failure of nerve. But a system of regular assemblies, or synods,

---

5. John Calvin to Cardinal James Sadoleto, 1 September 1539, Monergism, https://www.monergism.com/john-calvins-letter-cardinal-sadoleto-1539.

of pastors and elders at the local and regional levels decentralized church power and provided outlets for regular oversight of members and ministry. That model of church government caught on among Reformed Protestants undoubtedly because of the demographics of the Reformation. The difficult circumstances that Protestants, like Calvin himself, faced in their home countries forced them to migrate to centers that were open to refugees. Those who lived in Geneva while in exile, like Scotland's chief Reformer, John Knox, were amazed at the church reforms the city had achieved with Calvin's guidance.

The Necessity and Accomplishment of Reforming the Church

Three years after Calvin wrote his guidelines for church government, he prepared a treatise for a meeting of Charles V and the princes of the Holy Roman Empire at the German city of Speyer. The emperor was hoping to enlist the support of Lutheran and Calvinist princes in his war with France. It was a chance for Calvin to argue for the acceptance of Reformed Protestants as legitimate churches within the empire. His tract *The Necessity of Reforming the Church* divided the effort of Protestants into four categories. The first two were salvation and worship, which Calvin called the "soul" of the church. The other two, sacraments and church government, belonged to the church's "body." It was not a laundry list of Roman Catholic faults but a discerning look at what was important to Protestants, taking into consideration the poor state of Roman Catholicism. For Calvin the issue was not whether the church needed reform. Most Christians in Europe, especially its intellectuals and theologians, had agreed for the better part of two centuries that the church was guilty of mismanagement and immorality. The real question was how. And Calvin acknowledged that Luther began church reform with exactly the right question: "When God raised up Luther and others, who held forth a torch to light us into the way of salvation, and who, by their ministry, founded and reared our churches, those heads of doctrine in which the truth of our religion, those in which the pure and legitimate sonship of God, and those in which the salvation of men are comprehended, were in a great measure obsolete." Yet isolating the doctrine of salvation from worship, the sacraments, and church discipline was impossible. They were all connected: "We maintain that the use of the sacraments was in many ways vitiated and polluted. And we maintain that the government of the Church was converted into a species of foul and insufferable tyranny."[6]

The issue was which part of the church would start the reform. At one level the answer was obvious. Luther and German princes and then Swiss pastors and city magistrates had begun reformation. But who would carry it forward? Calvin detested the attitude of those who shrugged and said nothing could be done before blaming Protestants for dividing the church. Their opinion, he wrote, was that "the desperate condition of the Church makes it vain to attempt remedies, there being no hope of cure…. They…conclude that the best course is not to meddle with an evil well fixed." This attitude obviously denied that restoring the church was "the work of God" and did not depend on the "hopes and opinions of men" any more than "the resurrection of the dead." Calvin asserted, "It is the will of our Master that his gospel be preached. Let us obey his command." He also advised courage in the face of difficulty. He invoked the old proverb that "there is nothing illustrious which is not also difficult and arduous" to recommend fighting "through many difficulties." Calvin reminded the emperor of God's power. Surely those who hoped for church reform should desire the restoration of a faithful ministry at a level commensurate with their estimate of God and the importance of the church. Reformation was no trivial matter, and God was no being to take the church's ministry lightly.

Calvin did not change Charles's mind, nor did the reforms he recommended prevent the Council of Trent (1545–1563) from convening bishops from across Europe to condemn the proposals of Luther, Zwingli, Oecolampadius, Bucer, and Calvin, even as they recognized the deficiencies of bishops and priests and sought to redirect them toward greater faithfulness to church teaching. Even so, the

---

6. John Calvin, "The Necessity of Reforming the Church," Monergism, https://www.monergism.com/thethreshold/sdg/calvin_necessityreform.html.

bishops attached the words that Paul used regarding the Judaizers in Galatia—"Let them be anathema"—to Rome's rejection of Protestantism (see Gal. 1:8–9). To be sure, the council knew that reform was needed. The Counter-Reformation introduced measures to restore zeal and morality among clergy and laity. But rather than examining the structures that permitted abuses of office to persist or the theology that led church members to put their trust in the merits of saints, pray to saints, or venerate the host in the Mass, the Council of Trent allowed Roman Catholicism to continue its ways unreformed.

The result is that Roman Catholicism, even to this day, has not responded to the Protestant Reformers other than to reject the original tenets of Luther and Calvin. Some believe that recent cooperation between Protestants and Roman Catholics (e.g., Evangelicals and Catholics Together) is a sign that Rome has begun to take heed of Protestantism's zeal for the gospel. In point of fact, scandals continue to haunt the bishops and curia of Roman Catholicism (which suggests inherent flaws in episcopal structures of accountability), and the ambiguous acceptance of Protestant teaching is little more than liberal Roman Catholics and liberal Protestants recognizing that, for them, the sixteenth-century teachings that divided Protestants and Rome no longer have the significance they once did. In other words, not only did Rome never reform its ways but today's church has all the earmarks of the liberal Christianity that drove twentieth-century conservative Protestants to leave the mainline churches infected by modernism. Reformation is still the order of business for large sectors of the Protestant world. But it is especially pressing for Roman Catholics who have yet to reform the church.

That is why the Reformation is not a historical relic or anachronism. It still matters to anyone who cares about the gospel, worship that pleases God, a proper administration of the sacraments, and church government that assists believers in leading lives of holiness and righteousness.

2

SOLA SCRIPTURA

Protestantism started with Martin Luther's objections to the practice of indulgences, a feature of Roman Catholic ministry that most historians now concede had been seriously abused. According to Eamon Duffy, a Roman Catholic historian, the line that the Dominican preacher Tetzel used to solicit payment for indulgences was, "Place your penny on the drum, / the pearly gates open and in strolls mum." Duffy adds that "devout minds everywhere were revolted by this sort of stuff." And yet Pope Leo X was oblivious both to what was going on in German-speaking territories and to the abuses of Roman Catholic teaching. Again, Duffy provides perspective on the enormous gap between the papacy's geopolitical interests and what was happening in parishes throughout Europe: "The sophisticated Roman and Florentine worlds of classical learning and artistic patronage, the convoluted game of Italian dynastic politics in which the papacy must be a player if it was to survive at all, simply had not equipped [Leo X] to appreciate the more immediate and existential anxieties of the earnest."[1] Luther was simply a distraction.

The problem that Luther posed to the papacy became more apparent by 1520, when the controversy escalated from an abuse of church practice to one of legitimate authority. Leo's initial responses to Luther included having the monk's Augustinian superiors discipline him and taking away the political protection provided by Frederick of Saxony. When neither of these tactics worked, Leo issued *Exsurge*

---

1. Duffy, *Saints and Sinners*, 153, 154, 155.

Domine, a bull that condemned Luther's teaching on forty-one separate counts of heresy. Luther upped Leo's ante and burned the bull. He
said the papal condemnation was a "mere trifle."[2] From there Luther
appealed to German princes to reform the church since it was clear
that the papacy could not. Along the way, Luther shifted the rationale
for action. What tradition taught or what popes and councils ruled
was unimportant since those authorities could err—and had done so.
No, the real test for doctrine and ministry was the Bible. In his "Open
Letter to the Christian Nobility of the German Nation" (1520) Luther
wrote, "Since [popes] assert that the Holy Ghost has not deserted
them however ignorant and bad they may be, they venture to decree
just what they please." But, he added, "if this be so, what need or use
is there for Holy Scripture?"[3] In that exchange emerged the clas-
sic divide between Protestants and Roman Catholics—namely, the
Bible's authority versus the pope's.

   As many have observed, pitting a book against an office presents
its own difficulty since someone has to interpret the Bible. In addition, the Protestant idea of *sola Scriptura*, that the Bible alone—not
tradition, officers, or assemblies—is authoritative for what churches
do runs up against questions about the formation of the canon of
Scripture. These questions are like those about the chicken and the
egg. Did Scripture precede the church historically, or did the church
come before the formation of the Bible? Although these concerns
continue to absorb the attention of apologists for Roman Catholicism
and Protestant defenders of the sufficiency of Scripture, they were not
directly pressing at the time of the Reformation. For Luther and those
who rallied to his side, the real question was whether the papacy was
capable of overseeing the church in a way that was beneficial for the
spiritual needs of the faithful. For many in Europe, the limitations of
the papacy were obvious. It was an institution too big, too bloated,
and too much part of the political establishment to perform the

---

2. Martin Luther, quoted in Duffy, *Saints and Sinners*, 155.
   3. Martin Luther, quoted in Roland H. Bainton, "The Bible in the Reformation,"
in *The Cambridge History of the Bible*, vol. 3, *The West from the Reformation to the
Present Day* (New York: Cambridge University Press, 1963), 1.

needed work of Christian ministry. In that case, Protestants needed to find an authority for their convictions independent of the papacy. That authority was Scripture.

Biblical Authority

Luther and other Protestants did not concoct the idea of Scripture's infallibility and authority out of thin air for the sake of debate. The importance of Scripture had a long history in the church. In his book on *sola Scriptura*, Keith Mathison piles up quotations of the early church fathers' insistence on Scripture as the only rule, or standard, for the church. For instance, for the Latin father Tertullian, Scripture was the "absolute authority" and the constant basis by which he evaluated rival claims in doctrine and church life. He also thought the idea of tradition—that some of the apostles' authoritative teachings were handed down by word of mouth rather than in sacred text— ridiculous. Tertullian condemned as heretical the Gnostic idea that the apostles "proclaimed some and openly to all the world, whilst they disclosed others (only) in secret and to a few." Another prominent third-century theologian from the Latin West, Hippolytus, asserted, "There is, brethren, one God, the knowledge of whom we gain from the Holy Scriptures, and from no other source." In the fourth century, Cyril, bishop of Jerusalem, declared, "For concerning the divine and holy mysteries of the Faith, not even a casual statement must be delivered without the Holy Scriptures." So too, Augustine wrote about the authoritative status of the divine books of Scripture: "For holy scripture setteth a rule to our teaching that we dare not 'be wise more than it behoveth to be wise.'"[4]

Since the canon of Scripture was not finally recognized until the Council of Hippo in 393, one might well ask what these church fathers meant by "Holy Scriptures"? In fact, many of the fourth-century councils that determined the books of the New Testament were not ecumenical in nature. They were local and not binding on

---

4. Quoted in Keith Mathison, *The Shape of* Sola Scriptura (Moscow, Idaho: Canon Press, 2001), 25, 27, 31, 39.

the global church, and in many cases the determination concerned which sacred writings should be read in worship in addition to the Old Testament. For instance, Christian Smith argues that the church existed before the canon of Scripture, so the Bible actually depends on the authoritative decisions of bishops:

> With what scriptural authority did the Christian churches operate for their first 350 years, during which time they did not commonly possess the complete New Testament that Protestants today now claim is (along with the Old Testament) the necessary and only authority for Christian faith and practice?... And who or what actually authorized those bishops and theologians to even make those monumental decisions? How can evangelicals trust the New Testament itself—which exists in its received canonical form only and precisely because Catholic bishops and theologians met to define them?[5]

This is an argument that Roman Catholic apologists make often, even though it fails to acknowledge that technically Rome did not offer a binding definition of the canon until the sixteenth century with the Council of Trent. But it also comes with the failure to acknowledge that the bishops and theologians, even before 393, had a sense of a collection of sacred writings—beyond the Old Testament—that they called Scripture. Some lists vary on the New Testament writings. But the churches had an overwhelming consensus of a set of texts that were authoritative in a way akin to the Holy Scripture of the Old Testament saints.

Bruce Metzger's history of the formation of the New Testament reveals that the criteria for regarding a writing as sacred was not the bishops or council that drew up a list of books but the witness of Jesus and His apostles. He argues that the original sacred words were those of Jesus Himself, and collections of His sayings began to circulate that also formed the background for the gospel narratives. In addition to Jesus's words were the apostolic interpretations of Christ's teaching and activity, such as several of the early epistles of Paul. In the

---

5. Smith, *How to Go*, 42–43.

second and third centuries, Metzger adds, writings of bishops and theologians emerged that further reflected on the meaning and message of Christ's and the apostles' writings. At the same time, believers understood the difference between these later writings and the ones that bore the direct marks of Christ and the apostles. What further clarified the books that were canonical (authoritative and infallible) were heresies which arose, such as Marcionism, that challenged some of the books the church had regarded as sacred. As a result, a new "Christian canon" emerged that the church recognized as accompanying the Old Testament. This outcome was not the result of "a deliberate decree by an individual or council." Instead, it was a process shaped by "various kinds of influences and circumstances" that believers could explain only by referring to God's providential care for His church and the work of the Holy Spirit in the lives of Christians and the ministry of pastors.[6]

Important to notice as well in this debate between Protestants and Roman Catholics about the Bible versus tradition is that the notion of episcopal, conciliar, or papal authority did not drop out of the sky but also developed over time. This will be the topic of a later section in the book, but the idea that the church came before the Bible rarely considers that the authority of the church—especially the papacy—to which Roman Catholic apologists appeal was hardly clear in the first four centuries. Thus, Christian Smith's question could be posed in this way: How can Roman Catholics trust the bishops, who exist in their modern form only because they needed to defend and protect themselves from challenges to their authority? The early church did not have access to the Bible the way the contemporary church does. Nor did the early church witness Peter being inaugurated on the papal throne in St. Peter's Basilica. What is more, if the bishops were so competent to establish the books of the New Testament, and if they had such access to divine teaching by right of their episcopal authority, why would they decide to establish a biblical

---

6. Bruce M. Metzger, *The Canon of the New Testament: Its Origin, Development, and Significance* (Oxford: Clarendon Press, 1987), 7, 8.

canon? By forming the New Testament alongside the Old, the bishops and theologians established an authority that inherently challenged their own by collecting a set of writings by which to judge the church's ministers. It would have been much better for their sake and for their task of preventing error from arising in the church if they simply relied on their own deliberations, rulings, and teachings—better, that is, if the early church had not had a clear sense of a body of writings originating with Christ and the apostles which formed the standard for church teaching and decisions.

In the Middle Ages, Scripture retained its status as the incomparable source of divine truth. The Bible, of course, did not stand on its own. The study of Christian truth involved a number of other texts and considerations. For instance, theological investigation included the study of *sentences*, or scholarly considerations in abbreviated form of doctrinal and philosophical arguments relevant to a point under investigation. These sentences generally involved commentary on Scripture. Another factor that affected the Bible's authority was the canon itself and whether Scripture included the apocryphal books, which generally was the case throughout the later Middle Ages. In addition, the interpretation of the Bible often relied upon discerning the various senses of a text—its historical, moral, heavenly, and spiritual meanings. The Bible that scholars studied and that preachers used was the Vulgate, a Latin translation by Jerome that had its defects but that church authorities regarded as the standard for investigation. When the Renaissance, a rebirth of ancient learning, emerged in the fourteenth century, the effort to recover the original Greek and Latin texts of antiquity also facilitated an interest in the Hebrew and Greek behind the Latin text of the Vulgate. One last aspect of church life in the Middle Ages that affected the Bible's status was the authority of tradition, or a wider set of religious truths of which Scripture was part. Sometimes this tradition simply meant interpreting the Bible in the light of the received truths that the church had approved and continued to teach. In other cases, tradition included an awareness of teachings from Christ and the apostles not written down but passed on to the church that were now part of Christian truth. No matter how many hurdles of interpretation the study of Scripture needed to clear, underneath it all was a firm commitment to the Bible as the revealed will of God, apart from which the church could not depart without losing its way.

The medieval high regard for Scripture is evident in a couple of examples. The first is Thomas Aquinas's formulation of the relation between faith and reason. Notice that the greatest theologian of the Middle Ages, a doctor of the church, knows that reason (what can be known through nature) can go only so far in understanding God and that divine revelation is necessary to know and understand salvation:

> There is a two-fold mode of truth in what we profess about God. Some truths about God exceed all the ability of the human reason.... Beginning with sensible things, our intellect is led to the point of knowing about God that he exists, and other such characteristics that must be attributed to the First Principle. There are, consequently, some intelligible truths about God that are open to human reason; but there are others that absolutely surpass its power.[7]

Another example of the Bible's authority in the Middle Ages is the appeal to Scripture against the pope by fifteenth-century conciliarists, those who wanted to restrain and reform the papacy. Luther referred to Nicolo de Tudeschi, a Benedictine monk who eventually became archbishop of Palermo, who said during debates about papal authority, "In matters touching the faith, the word of a single private person is to be preferred to that of a pope if that person is moved by sounder arguments from the Old Testament and the New Testament."[8] Tudeschi's quotation is itself not authoritative, but it does show that believers and churchmen regarded the Bible as possessing an authority independent of ecclesiastical status or church law.

Luther's appeal to *sola Scriptura*, then, was neither unusual given the authority that the Bible had in the medieval church, nor was it

---

7. Thomas Aquinas, *Summa contra gentiles* (Notre Dame, Ind.: University of Notre Dame Press, 1957), 31.

8. Martin Luther, quoted in Bainton, "Bible in the Reformation," 2.

implausible given the circumstances he faced. Pope Leo X was simply one more example of a church officer who had lost the ability to distinguish his spiritual responsibilities from his political interests. This was the pope, who for financial reasons had appointed Albert of Brandenburg to three bishoprics simultaneously in return for twenty-five thousand gold florins. Albert had had to take out a loan to purchase his ecclesiastical offices. To pay off that loan, Leo gave Albert exclusive rights to sell the pope's plenary indulgences in the territories of Mainz and Brandenburg. Half the fee went to Albert, half to Leo. And Luther was supposed to assent to the spiritual discernment and authority of the papacy? Defenders of Roman Catholicism almost never acknowledge the self-interest that afflicted the Renaissance papacy as it tried to control the "spiritual" affairs of Christendom. Indeed, the appeal of Roman Catholicism to Protestants who convert is hard to square with how corrupt the church hierarchy had become by 1500 and how widely shared was the knowledge that the papacy did little for the spiritual well-being of the church or society. The Bible or the pope? For Luther, that was an easy decision, especially since no one in the medieval church questioned the Bible as a repository of divine truth and the message of salvation.

Bible Only: Its Meaning

Luther's appeal to the Bible against the pope, against the backdrop of the papacy's widely acknowledged failings, sounded at once both liberating and commonsensical. *Sola Scriptura* seemed to be a way to eliminate the papacy's stranglehold—many called it tyranny—on efforts to reform the church. It also made sense of medieval devotion and the high regard of the faithful for Scripture. The earth-shattering quality of asserting the Bible only was that it included a direct assault on the papacy. Here is how Luther put it in his "Open Letter to the Christian Nobility":

> With shameless words they conjure up the assertion that the pope cannot err in the faith, be he good or bad, and for this they adduce not a single letter [of Scripture].... They must admit that there are many among us, godly Christians, who have the true

faith, spirit, understanding, word and mind of Christ, and why then should one reject their word and understanding and follow the pope who has neither faith nor spirit.... Since we are all priests and all have one faith, one gospel, and one sacrament, why then should we not have the authority to test and determine what is right or not right in the faith? The word of Paul stands fast, I Corinthians ii, "A spiritual man judges all things and is judged of none."[9]

Over time, such reliance on Scripture as an infallible guide to salvation, as opposed to the words of fallible men and even church councils, emerged as a prominent feature of Protestant teaching.

In the earliest Lutheran and Reformed creeds, the authority of Scripture became a hallmark of Protestantism. For Lutherans, reliance on the testimony and authority of the Bible was everywhere implicit, but *sola Scriptura* did not become an article of faith in and of itself. For instance, in the Augsburg Confession (1530), an early Protestant confession addressed to the emperor from German nobles, the fourth article on justification uses Scripture as the basis for its teaching: "Also they teach that men cannot be justified before God by their own strength, merits, or works, but are freely justified for Christ's sake, through faith, when they believe that they are received into favor, and that their sins are forgiven for Christ's sake, who, by His death, has made satisfaction for our sins. This faith God imputes for righteousness in His sight. Rom. 3 and 4."

But in article 6 on new obedience, Augsburg invokes both Scripture and the church fathers—namely, Christ's teaching in Luke 17 and Ambrose. When Philip Melanchthon wrote a defense of the Augsburg Confession to respond to Protestantism's critics, he again used the Bible as an authority for Lutheran teaching, but the sufficiency of Scripture did not achieve confessional status per se. To the idea that church authorities had refuted Augsburg by appealing to the Bible, Melanchthon responded that they were in fact "far...from overthrowing our propositions by means of the Scriptures." Later in

---

9. Martin Luther, quoted in Bainton, "Bible in the Reformation," 2.

his defense, in article 15, Melanchthon again manifested the basic logic of Protestants—namely, that Scripture is always the final test for church teaching and ministry: "Whence are we rendered certain that rites instituted by men without God's command justify, inasmuch as nothing can be affirmed of God's will without God's Word? What if God does not approve these services? How, therefore, do the adversaries affirm that they justify? Without God's Word and testimony this cannot be affirmed."

For Reformed Protestants, however, the affirmation of biblical authority was explicit and emerged as an article of faith. For instance, the Ten Theses of Berne devoted its first two articles to Scripture:

1. The holy Christian Church, whose only Head is Christ, is born of the Word of God, and abides in the same, and listens not to the voice of a stranger.

2. The Church of Christ makes no laws and commandments without the Word of God. Hence human traditions are no more binding on us than they are founded in the Word of God.

Likewise, the Tetrapolitan Confession (1530), a creed that bore the fingerprints of Martin Bucer and that attempted to explain to the emperor the character of Protestantism in Reformed cities, began with an affirmation of Scripture as the basis for preaching and the reliable guide in a time of crisis: "The children of God everywhere, have always resorted—viz., to the authority of the Holy Scriptures" (ch. 1). The Gallican Confession of 1559, one of the earliest, fullest creeds of the Reformed churches, in this case the French church relying on Calvin in Geneva, devoted four of its first five chapters to revelation and scriptural authority, sandwiched by affirmations about God and the Trinity. In the fifth chapter, the French church confessed:

We believe that the Word contained in these books has proceeded from God, and receives its authority from him alone, and not from men. And inasmuch as it is the rule of all truth, containing all that is necessary for the service of God and for our salvation, it is not lawful for men, nor even for angels to

add to it, to take away from it, or to change it. Whence it follows that no authority, whether of antiquity, or custom, or
numbers, or human wisdom, or judgments, or proclamations,
or edicts, or decrees, or councils, or visions, or miracles, should
be opposed to these Holy Scriptures, but, on the contrary, all
things should be examined, regulated, and reformed according
to them. (ch. 5)

This had always been the appeal by Protestants—to go to a higher
authority than the church or the fathers, to go to the Word of God
itself. It was not a controversial move to appeal to the Bible. It was
to question the authority and tradition of the church. But for the
sake of an infallible authority, which made more sense? Did it make
more sense to appeal to church officials or theologians who were not
inspired by the Holy Spirit no matter how wise or godly they were, or
to appeal to the words that God had inspired? How much sense did
it make to appeal to the pope's authority when political interests may
have colored his judgments about the church's health and welfare?
Sola Scriptura was basic Christianity, and Protestants restored the
Bible, the very words where God's people find eternal life, to its place.

Of course, that was not how Roman Catholic authorities saw *sola
Scriptura*. At the Council of Trent, which convened over the course
of almost two decades due partly to war, plague, and imperial and
church politics, Rome had a chance to respond to the reforms for
which many called. During its first gathering of bishops and cardinals
from 1545 to 1549, more than thirty bishops addressed the subject of
Scripture, which included a host of questions: Were the apocryphal
books part of the canon? What about vernacular translations? How
much should preaching be based on the Bible? Just as important to
Rome was the question of tradition. As John O'Malley observes in his
history of the council, the church was hardly settled on what consti-
tuted its traditions since Rome had so many: doctrinal, disciplinary,
ecclesiastical, apostolic—some based in Scripture, some clearly without biblical basis. "Fasting on Friday? Infant baptism? The sign of the
cross? The observance of Sunday? Auricular confession," O'Malley
writes. "Are the decisions of previous councils traditions? What about

the writings of the Fathers?"[10] Protestants were hardly questioning a long and elaborate list of church teachings and practices since much within European Christianity was still in flux. What had given a measure of coherence to the church was papal authority and supremacy. Even though the pope had not contributed substantially to the teaching of the church the way theologians in Paris did, papal power set the terms for liturgy, ordination, and the sacraments. This was a form of influence on the laity, priests, monks, and nuns that even Thomas Aquinas never possessed. The papacy's ability to order the church had also become the problem—the papacy could give uniformity, but it could also abuse its power and distort the faith.

On the specific matter of *sola Scriptura*, participants at the council disagreed. Their problem in part was the clear statement by ancient and medieval theologians, as O'Malley concedes, who held "a Scripture-alone principle." In fact, the bishop of Chioggio, Jacopo Nacchianti, insisted that to put tradition on a par with Scripture was "impious."[11] Even so, the decree on Scripture asserted that God had revealed the gospel through "written books and unwritten traditions" that came from Christ Himself, the apostles, or the inspiration of the Holy Spirit. The decree also insisted that the Church of Rome had "preserved in unbroken sequence" the gospel of Christ and the apostles. Apparently the council thought that was a satisfactory response to Protestantism, notwithstanding that this language rejected implicitly the idea of *sola Scriptura*. But Pope Paul III wanted more reform than this, and Trent added decrees that required bishops to preach the gospel, even highlighting such proclamation as the bishop's chief task. That requirement in and of itself suggests that bishops were preoccupied with other duties and were not paying attention to Christ's instruction to Peter to "feed My sheep" (John 21:17). In that sense, the Council of Trent introduced its own blueprint for reform. Still, its decrees did nothing to challenge the authority of the

---

10. John W. O'Malley, *Trent: What Happened at the Council* (Cambridge, Mass.: Belknap Press of Harvard University Press, 2013), 92.

11. O'Malley, *Trent: What Happened at the Council*, 93, 95.

papacy or allow for Scripture to check the politics of the hierarchy. Also important to notice is that Trent did not simply take a different view of Scripture and tradition. The council also forbade the sort of appeal to Scripture that had launched the Reformation: "In order to restrain petulant spirits…no one, relying on his own skill, shall, in matters of faith, and of morals pertaining to the edification of Christian doctrine, wresting the sacred Scripture to his own senses, dare to interpret the said sacred Scripture contrary to that sense which is held by holy mother Church, whose it is to judge of the true sense and interpretation of the holy Scriptures." The council added that anyone found guilty of such interpretation would be "punished with the penalties by law established."[12]

The Bible versus Tradition in Practice

Although the Council of Trent actually made Scripture more prominent among Roman Catholics than it had been, the authority of the church and its traditions still obscured the Bible in Rome's system of teaching and practice. After the sixteenth century, the characteristic difference between Protestants and Roman Catholics was this: the former relied on the Bible, and the latter were under the authority of the church. This divergence became so typical that since the sixteenth century, Protestants and Roman Catholics could easily ridicule each other based on their allegiance either to Scripture or to the church. In the nineteenth-century United States, for instance, while Protestants established Bible societies to distribute Scripture, insisted on prayer and Bible reading in public schools, and established Sunday schools to increase literacy and knowledge of the Bible, Roman Catholics followed devotional practices that came from Rome with a heavy emphasis on the Sacred Heart (a picture of a heart with a crown of thorns), the Latin Mass, the Rosary, and accounts of miracles, such as apparitions of the virgin Mary. According to a leader of the Roman

---

12. "Decree Concerning the Edition, and the Use, of the Sacred Books," in *The Canons and Decrees of the Sacred and Oecumenical Council of Trent*, trans. J. Waterworth (London: Dolman, 1848), 19.

Catholic Redemptorist religious order, "We are children of the Church and of the truth; our adversaries are heretics or unbelievers; it is, then, our duty to take the offensive and to expose to the public the erroneous doctrines of Protestantism."[13] In effect, Trent had defeated Luther by keeping control of the Bible in the hands of the bishops and priests, in contrast to the Protestant churches and societies, in which translations and publication of Scripture made God's Word easily available to any person who could read.

A common complaint among Roman Catholics, especially converts from Protestantism, is that the church does not encourage knowledge of the Bible. At one Roman Catholic website, one writer laments that "Catholics are largely ignorant of the Bible." The reason is "the whole Counter-Reformation approach to Scripture that has characterized the Catholic Church for hundreds of years."[14] Another online article states, "Fifty years ago we did not have the Mass in English, a three-year lectionary cycle, or even a homily based on the gospel—rather they were based on Church teaching or practice. Before Vatican II 50 years ago, the Bible played a minimal role in the lives of most Catholics."[15] Even bishops in the United States admit that Roman Catholics have had trouble with the Bible:

> Up until the mid-twentieth Century, the custom of reading the Bible and interpreting it for oneself was a hallmark of the Protestant churches springing up in Europe after the Reformation. Protestants rejected the authority of the Pope and of the Church and showed it by saying people could read and interpret the Bible for themselves. Catholics meanwhile were discouraged from reading Scripture. Identifying the reading and interpreting of the Bible as "Protestant" even affected the study of Scripture.

13. Quoted in John T. McGreevy, *Catholicism and American Freedom: A History* (New York: W. W. Norton, 2004), 27.

14. "Catholics Don't Know the Bible," Make Church Matter, August 29, 2013, http://nativitypastor.tv/?p=1260.

15. Elizabeth Julian, "Vatican II and the Bible," *Wel*-Com, December 2, 2012, http://www.wn.catholic.org.nz/vatican-ii-and-the-bible/.

Until the twentieth century, it was only Protestants who actively embraced Scripture study.[16]

The Second Vatican Council attempted to change Roman Catholic attitudes toward the Bible. As Elizabeth Julian asserts, "Vatican II opened the Bible for Catholics" by recommending in *Dei Verbum* "easy access to Sacred Scripture" and by encouraging in the Constitution on Sacred Liturgy a "warm and living love for Scripture." Likewise, Daniel Kutys of the United States Conference of Catholic Bishops observes that the Second Vatican Council facilitated greater awareness of Scripture: "Mass was celebrated in the vernacular and so the Scripture readings at Mass were read entirely in English. Adult faith formation programs began to develop, and the most common program run at a parish focused on Scripture study."[17] The odd aspect of these changes in Roman Catholic devotional life, aside from how challenging it has been to nurture reading and study of Scripture, is that four hundred years after the Council of Trent, the Roman Catholic hierarchy has come around to the ideas that Luther and fellow Protestants proposed. In other words, even the Roman Catholic Church now concedes that the Bible should be central to the life and teaching of the church. Protestants knew that in the sixteenth century. If Rome refused that truth when proposed by the Reformers, it had less to do with Scripture as divine revelation than with protecting the prerogatives of bishops and cardinals, who at times worried more about the approval of princes and emperors than they did about the spiritual well-being of ordinary believers.

---

16. Daniel Kutys, "Changes in Catholic Attitudes toward Bible Readings," United States Conference of Catholic Bishops, http://www.usccb.org/bible/understanding -the-bible/study-materials/articles/changes-in-catholic-attitudes-toward-bible -readings.cfm.

17. Kutys, "Changes in Catholic Attitudes toward Bible Readings."

3

THE GOSPEL

The Reformation did not arrive in 1517 as a full-blown program for remedying the European churches' doctrine, worship, and government. It did begin, in the case of Martin Luther, with objections to abuses in the Roman Catholic Church. As both sides escalated their arguments, either to defend or question certain practices and the ideas that underwrote them, clear lines emerged that demarcated Protestantism and Roman Catholicism. That was even true of the material principle of the Reformation—justification by faith alone.

One indication of this doctrine's development was the religious disputation that the city council in Berne, Switzerland, called. Scheduled for January 1528, the event was part of the city government's attempt to calm increasing hostility between Roman Catholic cantons in the Swiss confederation with Zurich, where in 1522 Ulrich Zwingli had led reforms of church life in a Protestant direction. The event lasted three weeks, and the 250 theologians who attended—both proto-Protestant and Roman Catholic—used the Franciscan church in the city. The basis for debate was the Ten Theses of Berne, assembled from previous debates by Franz Kolbe and Berchthold Haller. In the end, two hundred theologians voted in favor of these Protestant-friendly assertions while forty-eight opposed them. Only one of the articles came close to the doctrine of justification by faith alone:

> 3. Christ is the only wisdom, righteousness, redemption, and satisfaction for the sins of the whole world. Hence it is a denial of Christ when we confess another ground of salvation and satisfaction.

Another clarified Christ's work as mediator, a point that bore on the doctrine of justification:

> 6. As Christ alone died for us, so he is also to be adored as the only Mediator and Advocate between God the Father and the believers. Therefore it is contrary to the Word of God to propose and invoke other mediators.

But the kind of precision that would later emerge in the French Confession of 1559 or the Heidelberg Catechism of 1563 was not evident among Protestants in the 1520s. In fact, Zwingli's Sixty-Seven Articles, produced in 1522 and Reformed Protestantism's earliest creed, never uses the word *justification*. The second article does summarize the gospel as "Christ, true Son of God," making known "the will of his heavenly Father," redeeming "us from death," and reconciling "us with God by his guiltlessness."

At the beginning of his controversy with Rome, not even Martin Luther had worked out precisely the nature of justification by faith alone. In his famous Ninety-Five Theses, for instance, the word *justification* does not appear, even though he attacks the theology that underwrote the sale of indulgences. Nor does the word *faith* emerge as one of Luther's assertions. In fact, the theses are much more about the nature of true repentance. The first is indicative: "When our Lord and Master Jesus Christ said, 'Repent' (Mt 4:17), he willed the entire life of believers to be one of repentance." Thirteen years later, when Lutheran theologians prepared a statement for Emperor Charles V that explained Protestantism, the fourth article on justification in the Augsburg Confession was short and showed the basic points of the doctrine: "Men cannot be justified before God by their own strength, merits, or works, but are freely justified for Christ's sake, through faith, when they believe that they are received into favor, and that their sins are forgiven for Christ's sake, who, by His death, has made satisfaction for our sins." Faith's function as the instrument by which believers receive Christ's righteousness came through in this brief assertion: "This faith God imputes for righteousness in His sight."

Many Europeans did not like their church. Calls for reform came from all quarters, even within the church. But only Protestants went beyond general calls for the church to adhere to its own standards of holiness to specific critiques of the theology that had nurtured Rome's abuses. And only Protestants produced a pastorally sensitive theology addressed to real fears that people had about sin, the demands of God's law, and the day of judgment. Perhaps those in positions of ecclesiastical authority might have been more flexible had not the need to preserve the church's hierarchy impeded reform. Certainly most of the pastors and theologians who led Protestantism had much less to lose by challenging the way Rome had "always" done things. Even so, arriving at a proper understanding of salvation required the give-and-take of critique, defense, and refinement. As much as Roman Catholics later came to the idea of the development of doctrine to explain that some truths took a while to emerge and become clear, development of doctrine was at the heart of Protestant origins as well. In fact, Western Christianity, because of Luther's initial challenge, developed two distinct accounts of how sinners become right with God, one Roman Catholic and one Protestant. Protestants formulated their understanding of justification by faith alone between 1520 and 1560. Rome responded at the Council of Trent between 1546 and 1563. Only then were the lines between Protestantism and Roman Catholicism clear.

The Problem with Indulgences

In 1845 John Henry Newman elaborated the idea of development of doctrine as a way to trace continuity within the changes to Rome's teachings. It was especially helpful for figuring out how, even if certain doctrines appeared to be in conflict with earlier teachings, they were still in continuity due to an ongoing and ever-expanding understanding of truth. In this sense, doctrine did not change; to admit such was to engage in contradiction. Instead, doctrine developed. Newman's notion may have been useful for thinking about papal encyclicals and the rulings of church councils between the Council of Trent and Vatican I (1870–1871), but it assumed too much coherence for the Roman Catholic Church prior to the sixteenth century. As much as the papacy gave a measure of order to Christianity in Western Europe, it did so largely administratively. Popes rarely taught, never wrote liturgies, and almost never issued catechisms that all bishops were supposed to use in their own dioceses. In other words, in 1500 Roman Catholicism did not represent merely one thing. Western Christianity between 1000 and 1500 was so ill-defined that abuses like those exhibited in the sale of indulgences were more likely to happen than not.

The Fourth Lateran Council (1215) was arguably the first time that the Roman Catholic Church composed a confession of faith between the ancient church's ecumenical councils (e.g., Nicaea and Chalcedon) and Trent. It was a busy council that attended to seventy-one items of business, from compensation for priests and the place of Jews in Christendom to a call for another crusade and even promises to believers who "take the cross and gird themselves up for the expulsion of heretics," the same indulgence "as is granted to those who go to the aid of the holy Land" (Constitution 3). The first item on the council's docket was a confession that, although brief, covered the high points of Roman Catholic teaching. The first of three paragraphs affirmed the Trinity, the body and soul of persons, and the reality of the devil and demons. The second paragraph explained the deity of Christ and His earthly ministry (being born of the "ever virgin Mary"), as well as His death, resurrection, ascension, and return on the last day.

The last paragraph of the Fourth Lateran Council was the only one that touched directly on matters of salvation. It asserted only one universal church, "outside of which nobody at all is saved." It went on to affirm the doctrine of transubstantiation, codified for the first time in official church teaching. This meant that Christ's "body and blood are truly contained in the sacrament of the altar under the forms of bread and wine, the bread and wine having been changed in substance, by God's power, into His body and blood." The council also addressed the subject of baptism, which apparently "anyone" could perform as long as he or she followed the "form laid down by the church." Baptism, the council instructed, "brings salvation to both children and adults." After being baptized, if Christians sinned, they needed to be restored "through true penitence." This simple and short paragraph gave the substance of Roman Catholic teaching on salvation, which continues for some to this day. In baptism a person is made alive to Christ and has original sin washed away. To remain in this state of salvation, church members need to perform acts of penance to receive forgiveness for venial sins and to receive absolution from priests for the guilt and penalty of mortal sins. In effect, baptism is initiation into the church, outside of which there is no salvation; the sacrament of penance, following confession of sins to a priest, is the remedy for ongoing sins; and the Mass is a participation in Christ by which Roman Catholics receive grace for forgiveness and the pursuit of godliness.

Alongside this meager formulation of salvation were teachings of popes and theologians about a period after life—purgatory—when deceased believers could become holy through either their own endurance of purgation or through the merits of other saints. Payment for the temporal penalty of sins was the reason for purgatory. For some reason, Christ's merits could apply to the eternal penalty for sin, but transgressions against persons or social institutions were not covered by Christ's mercy. As a result, the church began in the Middle Ages to develop the idea of a treasury of merits, those of Christ and saints, which could apply to believers who were alive. Only in the fifteenth century did church officials begin to extend the merits of Christ and the saints to the deceased—in other words, those in purgatory. This was the origin of the system of indulgences to which Luther objected. The laity could pay for indulgences for either themselves or their deceased loved ones as a thank offering to the church for its ministry. In 1343 Pope Clement VI had issued a statement, *Unigenitus*, which regularized the system of indulgences, not only stipulating the prices but also spiritual requirements like prayer and acts of penance, thereby giving the practice papal approval. In Luther's day, indulgences became an outgrowth of the doctrine of purgatory, and the buying and selling of indulgences became a big business in the years leading up to the construction of St. Peter's Basilica in Rome.

John Tetzel made a career of selling indulgences.[1] He had begun to make them available as early as 1502, and by 1517 Pope Leo X had commissioned Tetzel as the chief administrator of indulgences for the German-speaking territories in Europe. Reliable historical evidence shows that the proceeds from the indulgences Tetzel was selling were paying both for St. Peter's Basilica in Rome and for the archbishopric that Prince Albert of Brandenburg had purchased from Pope Leo X. Tetzel never entered Luther's hometown of Wittenberg because the local ruler, Frederick the Wise, had barred the preacher. But people from Wittenberg were traveling to hear Tetzel and buy indulgences, developments that drove Luther to craft his Ninety-Five Theses, which included the following:

27. They preach only human doctrines who say that as soon as the money clinks into the money chest, the soul flies out of purgatory.

28. It is certain that when money clinks in the money chest, greed and avarice can be increased; but when the church intercedes, the result is in the hands of God alone.

In popular conceptions of the Reformation, after the Ninety-Five Theses the rest is history. In fact, Luther had already preached

---

1. According to the contemporary Roman Catholic catechism, Q. 1471, "An indulgence is a remission before God of the temporal punishment due to sins whose guilt has already been forgiven, which the faithful Christian who is duly disposed gains under certain prescribed conditions through the action of the Church which, as the minister of redemption, dispenses and applies with authority the treasury of the satisfactions of Christ and the saints." It is "partial or plenary according as it removes either part or all of the temporal punishment due to sin." The catechism also states that indulgences "may be applied to the living or the dead." The catechism goes on to teach that a Christian may obtain an indulgence "through the Church who, by virtue of the power of binding and loosing granted her by Christ Jesus, intervenes in favor of individual Christians and opens for them the treasury of the merits of Christ and the saints to obtain from the Father of mercies the remission of the temporal punishments due for their sins." Because Rome teaches that those in purgatory are "members of the same communion of saints," living Christians may help the deceased by obtaining indulgences for them, "so that the temporal punishments due for their sins may be remitted" (Q. 1478–79).

three sermons against indulgences the year prior to his points of disputation. He had asserted then that remission of even temporal punishments could never be certain in the case of the dead since remission depended on worthy contrition and confession and no one, not even the pope, could know of a deceased person's sincerity. Luther also claimed that if the pope had the power to grant indulgences to the dead, a notion that the Reformer believed to be highly dubious, then he was cruel not to grant indulgences to all those Christians in purgatory. Finally, Luther argued that buying and selling indulgences was self-defeating since the transactions undermined the piety— true confession and contrition—that the sacrament of penance was designed to promote.

For Luther, indulgences were just the tip of the iceberg of deficiencies in the Roman Catholic Church. Linked as they were to the sacrament of penance, indulgences highlighted how much Rome was in flux in its understanding of salvation. That sinners needed to atone for their sins was clear. How they were to do this and how dependent a believer's actions were on grace and, specifically, the work of Christ was uncertain, even within a communion where the papacy had increasingly centralized and consolidated ecclesiastical administrative structures. In other words, Luther and Tetzel were at odds, but rivalries and disputes such as this were common in the Roman Catholic Church, in which, prior to the Council of Trent, the teachings and practices of those dioceses in communion with the bishop of Rome varied.

Abuses in the sale of indulgences raised further questions about Rome's teaching on salvation. As meager as infallible teachings by pope and councils may have been compared to the actual teachings of theologians at universities or of intellectuals in the religious orders, Rome's account of salvation on the eve of the Reformation featured the institutional church as the dispenser of grace, with priests ordained by bishops, who were appointed by the pope, who was preceded by apostles administering the sacraments of baptism, penance, and the Mass. As the historical circumstances of sixteenth-century Germany indicate, the laity's thirst for satisfaction from the penalty of venial sins produced the sort of commercial traffic in indulgences that drew Luther's ire against Tetzel. Add to this the designs of princes and popes for raising revenues, and you have a system ripe for both spiritual abuse and fiscal malfeasance. Even the *New Catholic Encyclopedia*'s entry on indulgences concedes that Rome's teaching on indulgences is susceptible to abuse:

> The popularity of indulgences contributed no small part to the welfare of medieval society. Thanks to indulgences in the form of material and monetary gifts, great cathedrals and monastic establishments were built and kept in repair, schools and universities were founded and endowed, hospitals were maintained and bridges were built.... In spite of this, abuses in the granting and preaching of indulgences were not slow to appear. Bishops multiplied indulgences, and preachers exaggerated their efficacy. When indulgences were granted for monetary gifts, as for the upkeep of churches or the building of new ones, the collectors...often received more money than was due, thus paying themselves for their work. In addition, not all the money was used for the purpose for which the indulgence was preached.

By 1567 Rome recognized the problem and outlawed the sale of indulgences. But in 2000 Pope John Paul II encouraged bishops to recover the practice of granting indulgences as part of the observance of the new millennium.

To boil the Reformation down to the tawdry case of building cathedrals and funding benefices on the backs of ordinary persons' desire for forgiveness of sins is simplistic, but the practice of indulgences and its relevant teaching did expose Rome's serious deficiency and the potential for mixed motives complicating the ministry of forgiveness. Luther bore the burden for most of the early years of the Reformation. To be sure, throughout the faculties and among many of the clergy of the sixteenth century was a sense that Rome needed to be reformed. Humanists such as Erasmus and Thomas More were readily aware of the abuses of the Renaissance popes, the worldliness of clergy in the pursuit of status and influence, and the hypocrisy of priests and monks who taught Christian virtues but failed to practice what they preached. Still, no one so openly and publicly questioned Rome's teaching on salvation as Luther did. His exposition of the fall, sin, Christ's death and resurrection, and faith opened the door for many more Western Christians to reexamine Scripture and the early church and see whether Rome had abandoned the message of Christ and the apostles. Out of the ferment that Luther provoked came the first stirrings of Reformed Protestantism.

Debates over Justification

Although Protestants took time to develop their own definition of justification, by 1536 a consensus had emerged that Lutherans shared with Reformed Protestants. According to the First Helvetic Confession (1536), the creed composed by pastors from Swiss cities, Christ's satisfaction of God's demands for the punishment of sin and a life of perfect holiness were the basis for a believer's righteousness: "We do not obtain such sublime and great benefits of God's grace and the true sanctification of God's Spirit through our merits or powers but through faith which is a pure gift of God." The authors went on to explain that love and all other virtues and good works are not part of faith itself but the fruit of faith. "Although this faith effects innumerable good works, it does not take comfort in them but in the mercy of God." This was a significant clarification for recent discussions on justification between Roman Catholics and Protestants in the United States since many of the joint declarations have included love or charity as part of genuine faith, a fusion that the Reformers went out of their way to deny. To join faith and love was to confuse Christ's perfect righteousness with the good works of a Christian, as if a believer's virtues earned Christ's merits. As the Geneva Confession (1536), a creed largely written by Calvin, explained, "In order that all glory and praise be rendered to God (as is his due), and that we be able to have true peace and rest of conscience, we understand and confess that we receive all benefits from God, as said above, by his clemency and pity, without any consideration of our worthiness or the merit of our works."

Some Roman Catholics were willing to consider Protestants' teaching. Political considerations within the Holy Roman Empire were a factor. The Emperor Charles V needed unity among Christians to prosecute his war against the Ottomans, who were invading Europe from the East. One of the most significant gatherings of Roman Catholics and Protestants came in 1541 at the Diet of Regensburg. Here, leaders on each side of the debate, including Martin Bucer, Philip Melanchthon, Johannes Eck, and Gasparo Contarini, met to discuss the most contentious points raised by Protestants—from the fall and original sin to ecclesiastical authority and the sacraments. In the larger scheme of church history, Regensburg revealed a brief period when political and ecclesiastical authorities were willing to conduct discussions with Protestants despite previous papal imperial condemnations of Martin Luther at the Diet of Worms (1521). Undoubtedly, the reasons for holding these deliberations were not simply spiritual. Hopes for maintaining social and religious order within Europe were also at play. At the same time, the failure of Regensburg to achieve consensus was an important aspect of Pope Paul III's decision in 1545 to convene the Council of Trent, a body that clearly rejected compromise and condemned Protestant teaching.

Even so, the debates over justification at Regensburg are valuable for clarifying what the Reformation taught and why Rome could not tolerate Protestantism. On the first four points—human nature before the fall, free will, the cause of sin, and original sin—the participants agreed. On the fifth point, justification, both sides also seemed to agree, though reactions to the proposed language suggested that the agreement could be read a variety of ways. Regensburg attempted to consolidate Protestant and Roman Catholic understandings of justification by speaking of a twofold righteousness in the reality of a sinner being justified. For Protestants the notion of an imputed or alien righteousness—namely, Christ's—received by faith alone was one part of Regensburg's assertion. For Roman Catholics, an inherent righteousness or holiness wrought within the justified person was imperative. The Protestant position held that justification does not arise from something a sinner does to become acceptable to God. Such acceptance was impossible because of the devastating effects of sin. Roman Catholics, conversely, believed that sinners become acceptable to God by becoming righteous in themselves, not on their own but through God's gracious work in the life of a believer. The compromise attempted at Regensburg was to affirm that justification included both forms of righteousness—inherent and imputed. In addition, while Regensburg taught that God accepts a sinner because of the merits of Christ a believer receives in faith, this also included the gift of the Spirit, who worked in the Christian a hatred of sin, repentance, and love. In effect, Regensburg attempted to combine both justification and sanctification under the doctrine of justification; in contrast, Lutherans and Reformed Protestants would go on to distinguish justification as a forensic declaration and sanctification as moral renovation, two distinct though simultaneous benefits of salvation.

The attempted harmony of Protestant and Roman Catholic views was largely responsible for the confusion that Regensburg created and its ultimate rejection. John Calvin wrote to his colleague William Farel of his surprise to see Rome give up so much on the idea of imputed righteousness. Calvin added that he believed the statement was insufficiently clear. Martin Luther, in contrast, judged that affirming justification by faith alone and justification by faith working through love was "thrown" and "glued together."[2] The chief source of confusion was failure to distinguish a life of dying to sin (sanctification) from justification proper. Regensburg was not as great a concession for Protestants—hence Calvin's reaction—since they believed that justification and sanctification always went together in a person who trusted the promises of the gospel. For Roman Catholics to accept the idea of imputed righteousness was much more difficult since it was, as the Council of Trent would prove, at odds with Rome's emerging consensus on salvation.

---

2. Martin Luther, quoted in Anthony N. S. Lane, "A Tale of Two Imperial Cities: Justification at Regensburg (1541) and Trent (1546–1547)," in Bruce L. McCormack, *Justification in Perspective: Historical Developments and Contemporary Challenges* (Grand Rapids: Baker Academic, 2006), 123–24.

Just as hard for Roman Catholics were Protestant convictions about abiding sin in the believer and the status of good works. Although Regensburg conceded that sin remained in a Christian after conversion, it was not as clear as Protestant confessions would be on the tainted nature of a believer's good works on account of the remnants of sin. The Protestant understanding of good works insisted that even a Christian's best efforts failed to meet God's righteous standards. God did indeed accept a believer's good works as good but only because He viewed them through the perfect righteousness of Christ.

The chief difficulty for Protestants with Regensburg was the idea of justifying faith working through love. This idea was at odds with the notion of faith alone. Faith working through love suggested that faith was a form of good works and therefore played a role in meriting God's favor and bestowing more grace. The Reformers did believe that faith is always accompanied in the Christian by an infusion of love. At the same time, they insisted on distinguishing between faith and love (just as they distinguished between justification and sanctification) so as not to confuse good works or the best intentions of repentant sinners with the righteousness of Christ, which alone could meet God's perfect standard of holiness. According to Anthony N. S. Lane, Regensburg's "statements that we are justified on the basis of *efficacious* faith and that faith is effectual through love *could* be taken to mean that justification is on the basis not of faith alone" but by a faith "formed by love." He adds, "Thus it was claimed by some Roman Catholics at Regensburg that the article [on justification] taught justification by *love* alone."[3]

By the middle of the sixteenth century, Protestant and Roman Catholic opposition on justification had clarified to the point that each side rejected the other as a repudiation of the gospel. In 1559 the Reformed churches of France, in the Gallican Confession, affirmed justification in a way that underscored the importance of imputation: "We believe that all our justification rests upon the remission of our sins, in which also is our only blessedness, as saith the Psalmist

---

3. Lane, "Tale of Two Imperial Cities," 128.

(Ps. 32:1). We therefore reject all other means of justification before God, and without claiming any virtue or merit, we rest simply in the obedience of Jesus Christ, which is imputed to us as much to blot out all our sins as to make us find grace and favor in the sight of God" (art. 18). Two years later, Guido de Bres wrote the Belgic Confession for the churches in the Low Countries, which linked salvation with imputation and faith alone:

> We believe that our salvation consists in the remission of our sins for Jesus Christ's sake, and that therein our righteousness before God is implied, as David and Paul teach us, declaring this to be the happiness of man, that God imputes righteousness to him without works. And the same Apostle saith, that we are justified freely by his grace, through the redemption which is in Jesus Christ. And therefore we always hold fast this foundation... relying and resting upon the obedience of Christ crucified alone, which becomes ours when we believe in him. This is sufficient to cover all our iniquities, and to give us confidence in approaching God; freeing the conscience of fear, terror, and dread, without following the example of our first father, Adam, who, trembling, attempted to cover himself with fig-leaves. (art. 23)

In contrast, the bishops who met at the Council of Trent rejected and condemned Protestant teaching on justification. In its Sixth Session (1547), Trent defined justification as both "remission of sins" and "sanctification and renewal of the inward man," combined with the "voluntary reception of the grace and gifts whereby an unjust man becomes just." For Rome, justification was a process. For Protestants it was a forensic declaration. The instrument by which a person was justified, according to Trent, was baptism, "the sacrament of faith," thus tying salvation to the rites of the church more than to the work of the Spirit in generating saving faith. Although Trent did highlight the importance of faith in regard to justification, it was not faith alone but faith along with hope and love. In fact, justification, for Roman Catholics, required an infusion of charity in the soul of a believer:

> For though no one can be just except he to whom the merits of
> the passion of our Lord Jesus Christ are communicated, yet this
> takes place in that justification of the sinner, when by the merit
> of the most holy passion, the charity of God is poured forth
> by the Holy Ghost in the hearts of those who are justified and
> inheres in them; whence man through Jesus Christ, in whom
> he is ingrafted, receives in that justification, together with the
> remission of sins, all these infused at the same time, namely,
> faith, hope and charity. (Council of Trent, Sixth Session)

In other words, while Protestants identified justification with the righteousness of Christ imputed to the believer through the instrument
of faith, Roman Catholics located justification in a constellation of
activities—some the work of God, some the virtues of a Christian—
and so obscured a believer's dependence on Christ's work alone for
salvation. In fact, Trent made that obscurity explicit when it affirmed
"faith, unless hope and charity be added to it, neither unites man
perfectly with Christ nor makes him a living member of His body."
Faith alone could not save but required other virtues in the Roman
Catholic system. This allowed Trent also to connect works to faith: "It
is most truly said that faith without works is dead and of no profit…
faith that worketh by charity." Not only did Trent's teaching on justification undermine the efficacy of Christ's righteousness but it also
refused to let faith alone stand as the instrumental means by which a
Christian obtained Christ's mercy. Faith inherently involved love for
it to be effective, so that faith with some sort of good works attached
was the way Rome responded to Protestantism's insistence on faith
alone. What is more, Trent's teaching was not merely a counterpro-
posal. It was definitive: "If anyone says that the sinner is justified by
faith alone, meaning that nothing else is required to cooperate in
order to obtain the grace of justification, and that it is not in any way
necessary that he be prepared and disposed by the action of his own
will, let him be anathema." So ended Protestant and Roman Catholic
discussions of justification for the next four hundred years.

Does the Debate Still Matter?

But a funny thing happened on the road from the Second Vatican Council (1962–1965). When the bishops and cardinals who met in Rome to update Roman Catholicism decided to enter into ecumenical relationships with other Christians, their rationale was that Protestants were "separated" siblings, believers who did not have the fullness of Rome's teaching and practice but who nonetheless worshiped and believed in the true God. Although their teaching had once been worthy of anathema, Protestants who taught justification by faith alone were now worthy of respect and even admiration.

Although Rome's new attitude toward Protestantism seemed to be a replay of the kind of doctrinal indifference that conservative Protestants had detected in early twentieth-century liberal Protestantism, since the Second Vatican Council, popes and the curia have pursued negotiations with other Christian communions, from the Orthodox in the East to Anglicans in the West. Among those ecumenical discussions were meetings between Rome and the Council of the Lutheran World Federation, which produced in 1999 the Joint Declaration on the Doctrine of Justification. In his apologia for becoming a Roman Catholic, Christian Smith advises other would-be converts that they need to become familiar with this "world-historical religious event," the time when Rome ended "its core historical disagreements with Lutheranism."[4] Never mind that the Lutheran church body with whom Rome deliberated is one that ordains women, does not recognize the primacy of the papacy, and refuses to condemn what had previously been regarded sin (divorce, homosexuality, and sex outside marriage). In other words, Rome was not reconsidering the doctrine of justification with those Lutherans who still care about the differences that led to the Reformation. The Vatican was more comfortable carrying on discussions with liberal Protestants than with conservatives, even Lutherans that ordain women and bless gay marriages.

Smith also fails to notice that the Joint Declaration says nothing really about the original Protestant teaching about faith alone or the

---

4. Smith, *How to Go*, 81.

imputed righteousness of Christ. To be sure, the catechism produced by John Paul II affirms "grace alone"—but so did Trent. The question is whether justification comes from faith alone or whether faith needs the help of love and hope (read "cooperation"). Not to be missed in the Joint Declaration is that both sides still disagree about justification. Even these liberal Lutherans still insist that justification is by faith alone, though they fail to affirm the alien righteousness of Christ imputed to sinners by faith: "In faith they place their trust wholly in their Creator and Redeemer and thus live in communion with him." In contrast, in the next paragraph, Roman Catholics insist that "in justification the righteous receive from Christ faith, hope, and love and are thereby taken into communion with him." For Lutherans faith is still singular while for Roman Catholics faith is alongside hope and love. At the same time, the liberal Lutherans distinguished still between justification (declaration of righteousness) and sanctification (moral renewal). In the doctrine of justification by faith alone, "a distinction but not a separation is made between justification itself and the renewal of one's way of life that necessarily follows from justification." Meanwhile, according to the Joint Declaration, Roman Catholics still regard justification as sanctification: "[Roman] Catholic teaching emphasizes the renewal of life by justifying grace," and "this renewal in faith, hope, and love is always dependent on God's unfathomable grace.... The justification of sinners is forgiveness of sins and being made righteous by justifying grace, which makes us children of God." The ambiguity of this "historic" statement is inherent in statements that reflect ongoing discussions, though for some the Joint Declaration is the final word that settles the Reformation debates (see paragraphs 26 and 27).

Even so, modern theological discussions, long removed from the desire for and methods of systematic theology, cannot resolve the standoff between Rome and Protestantism unless each side actually comes to the table believing what its theological ancestors believed. As Lane observes about the joint statement, the Joint Declaration renders the doctrine of imputed alien righteousness in a weakened form as "forgiveness/non-imputation of sin, a concept that Catholics have always held." He adds, "This failure to acknowledge a key element of the traditional Protestant doctrine is a serious omission."[5] This is not simply a failure to do justice to sixteenth-century ideas. It is a failure of people who presume to minister Christ's word and carry on the work of Christ's apostles to be clear about how sinners become right with God. If humans have any hope to overcome the depths of sin that clings to all descendants of Adam, they need a perfect righteousness that comes only from Christ's obedience to all God's law and His satisfaction on the cross of God's punishment of sin. Infused righteousness by "grace alone" might sound like it removes human effort, but it does not have a remedy for indwelling sin, which is why so many Roman Catholics will wind up in purgatory, according to Rome's historic teaching. The only way that believers can stand innocent before God on judgment day is by wearing the garments of Christ's perfect righteousness. That was the insight and achievement of the Protestant Reformation. Rome may no longer oppose that belief the way it used to. But it has yet to reform its teachings and practices, which make its members still dependent on the works of saints and acts of penance and less hopeful about going to be with the saints and angels at death.

5. Lane, "Tale of Two Imperial Cities," 126.

4

WHY CHURCH GOVERNMENT MATTERS

Ask any resident of Europe or North America about the value of monarchy, and chances are you will hear doubts about rule by a single hereditary head of state. Liberalism has become so synonymous with democracy that monarchy sounds like a relic of the feudal past. Yet constitutional monarchies still exist in places where Reformed churches have thrived—the United Kingdom and the Netherlands, for instance. Even so, the functions of kings or queens are mainly ceremonial, so that affection for monarchy as a system of government is merely a personal preference, on the order of liking French Roast more than Sumatra in your coffee mug or Bach more than Elgar in your playlist. The revolutions of the late eighteenth century in North America and France challenged the assumed superiority of rule by one that had dominated the West since Emperor Constantine converted to Christianity. Ever since the French Revolution began in 1789, governments in the West, or those wanting to modernize, implement polities that take power out of the hands of a single sovereign and disperse authority among popularly elected officials who govern within the limits of constitutional provisions ratified by "the people."

In church government, however, rule by one is far more common than rule by the few (presbyterianism) or the many (congregationalism). Anglican communions still rely on the archbishop of Canterbury (senior to the junior archbishop of York), while at the local level diocese bishops or archbishops preside over church life. As hierarchical as Anglicanism might seem to Congregationalists or Presbyterians, the Roman Catholic Church represents an older style of divine-right monarchy that even Anglican archbishops refuse to claim. The bishop of Rome, also known as the pope, is the sole head of a worldwide communion that includes over one billion church members. To be sure, the pope has a large bureaucracy in the Vatican to assist in the oversight of dioceses, orders, universities, hospitals—the list could go on—all over the world. But the papacy's authority is unquestioned and unrivaled. Papal theory teaches not only that the bishop of Rome is infallible when teaching on matters of faith and morality but also emphatically affirms that as the successor to Peter, the apostle Christ apparently designated as the rock of the church, the bishop of Rome is superior in power, stature, and teaching to every other bishop in the world. Such authority explains why the inauguration ceremony for a new pope resembles the rites that Europeans have long used when coronating a new king.

And yet the claims of papal authority did not begin with Peter and the apostles. Papal supremacy emerged only after many historical circumstances (and even then the effectiveness of the papacy was never obvious), not simply for preserving church unity but also as a means of pastoral care. In fact the failures of the papacy produced a crisis in the medieval church that provided the backdrop for Protestants to propose church reforms that replaced episcopacy with forms of church government not simply more biblical but also more responsive to the needs of the laity. By decentralizing ecclesiastical power, and in the case of Reformed and Presbyterian churches, by establishing oversight by elders and pastors (presbyters), the Reformation went beyond reforms of doctrine and worship to tackle one of the chief obstacles to any kind of effort to improve the witness and work of the church—namely, the papacy. What the Reformers came to understand was that without the proper structures of church governance, reformation would be partial and temporary at best.

Problem with the Papacy

One of the ironies in many Protestant-to-Roman Catholic conversion stories is the prominence of the papacy as a powerful and consoling alternative to the denominationalism of evangelicals. For instance, in *Catholic Converts and Conversion*, Dave Armstrong contends that without a central authority, Christianity lacks unity. "People may wish to war against infallibility or the papacy," he writes.[1] But Christians still need some kind of authority (as if the Bible is not authoritative or infallible). Unless the papacy's decrees are binding, Christians may always "dissent," which leads to the disagreements among Protestants and their lack of unity. That understanding looks pretty good on paper, though whether it is better than the infallibility of Scripture is another matter. Some converts complain that an infallible Bible still needs an infallible interpreter. What they seem to forget (especially if they do not follow press coverage of Pope Francis) is that papal statements also find a host of interpretations, so that bishops today are not united on whether divorce and remarriage disqualifies a Roman Catholic from receiving Communion. When it came to papal authority at the time of the Reformation, the problems of the papacy were precisely what drove many Reformers and humanists to look to other ecclesiastical authorities to rein in a bishop of Rome who either was oblivious to the demands for holiness or was caught up in the rivalries of European politics, or both.[2]

When Martin Luther questioned the sale of indulgences and defended himself by appealing to the authority of Scripture, he also requested help from the German nobility. His call for the lords and magistrates of the German-speaking lands to reform the church was closely linked to the doctrine of the priesthood of all believers and the Protestant idea of vocation—serving God in one's secular work (see chapter 5). Luther also invoked the authority of church councils against the papacy in his "Open Letter to the Christian Nobility of the German Nation." That pamphlet spoke directly to the barriers (i.e., "three walls") the papacy had erected to protect itself from

---

1. Dave Armstrong, *Catholic Converts and Conversion* (self-pub., 2013), 44.

2. Legendary Pope Alexander VI (1492–1503), for instance, not only continued the papacy's obsession with European politics but led a dissolute life that included affairs with several mistresses and ecclesiastical and political appointments for his illegitimate children. Alexander's conduct in office was not unusual for the Renaissance papacy (roughly 1417–1521).

reform. The first two obstacles were the idea that the civil realm had no jurisdiction over the spiritual and that only the papacy had the authority to interpret Scripture in a definitive manner. The last wall that Luther hoped to topple was the claim that only a pope could call a council of bishops. On the one hand, he wrote, theologians and churchmen "have no basis in Scripture for their contention that it belongs to the pope alone to call a council or confirm its actions."[3] This system was rigged if the pope himself needed to be called to account. Would he actually call for a council to accuse himself or to correct his own teaching? That was not, Luther argued, how the early church operated when it called the Council of Jerusalem and did not wait for the alleged first pope, Peter, to call the assembly. Nor was it the way Paul handled Peter's error when the former opponent of the church confronted Peter "to his face" about a faulty understanding of the gospel (Gal. 2:11–13). On the other hand, the example of the first ecumenical council, Nicaea (325), the assembly that set the pattern for Trinitarian orthodoxy, indicated that civil magistrates could call church councils since the bishops there gathered at Emperor Constantine's request. For church reform to occur, Luther hoped for a church council (rule by the few) because episcopacy (rule by one) was incapable of reforming itself.

Luther undoubtedly had history in mind when he appealed to the German nobility to call a church council because roughly one hundred years before his church troubles, an assembly of bishops had gathered to rescue the papacy from the gravest crisis of the Western church's institutional authority. Apologists for Roman Catholicism like to talk about the continuity of church history and the unity and authority that the papacy ideally supplies to the Roman communion, but they conveniently overlook the defects of episcopacy that became apparent to most Christians in the opening decades of the fifteenth century. Even Brad Gregory, whose popular book *The Unintended*

---

3. Martin Luther, "An Open Letter to the Christian Nobility of the German Nation," trans. C. M. Jacobs, in *Works of Martin Luther* (1915; repr., Grand Rapids: Baker, 1982), 2:77.

Reformation: How a Religious Revolution Secularized Society blames most of modern society's worst features (consumerism, materialism, and relativism) on processes that Protestantism began, has to concede that Rome's coveted institutional authority had brought Western Christianity to the edge of destruction. He observes that after the eleventh century, when the papacy began to consolidate its authority in Europe, a chasm between Christian ideals and papal practice emerged such that individual popes at different times emerged as reformers who called the bishops back to their true spiritual calling (Gregory VII and Leo IX in the eleventh century and Innocent III in the twelfth). Instead of following the example of Jesus and "stripping themselves of pride and pretense," Gregory admits, most popes "defended the status quo" or made the papacy worse. By the fourteenth century, when the papacy's institutional vigor was sufficient to influence European politics, the immorality and decadence that came with the political power of popes was even more evident for devoted believers to see. Even Benedict XII, a Cistercian monk who attempted to avoid Rome's corruption by moving the papacy to Avignon, took up residence in a large papal palace that evoked privilege and power more than service and sacrifice.[4]

The relocation of the papacy to Avignon (1309–1377) indicated the influence of secular authorities on the episcopal successor to Peter (in this case the French monarchy), but it was also a problem for those who looked to the papacy for making the church one. From 1377 until 1417, two popes vied for authority in the Western church, one in Avignon and one in Rome. This was the period of the Western Schism, and reestablishment of the papacy in Rome during this period was a well-intended effort to liberate the pope from subservience to the French crown. But it also left the church with two popes and almost no possibility of an easy resolution (or a ready argument for papal power). The only way out was a church council. Indeed,

---

4. Brad S. Gregory, *The Unintended Reformation: How a Religious Revolution Secularized Society* (Cambridge, Mass.: Belknap Press of Harvard University Press, 2012), 41.

conciliarism was one of the proposals that some churchmen advocated as a way around popes who seemed to be unaccountable, and eventually it became the preferred form of church government for Protestants, with the exception of Anglicans. The Council of Constance, a body of bishops and cardinals, met off and on between 1414 and 1418 to address the crisis within the church hierarchy. This was by no means a proto-Protestant body since this council also condemned Jan Hus, a Czech priest who objected to Rome's defects in ways that anticipated Luther. The council also reaffirmed an earlier condemnation of John Wycliffe, another forerunner of the Reformation. These decisions indicate that the Council of Constance was not a place for challenging church tradition. But the crisis of the papacy was so severe that, as Gregory admits, the bishops not only deposed the existing popes in Avignon and Rome but "departed strikingly from long-standing church governance" by declaring councils superior to popes.[5] The pope they elected, Martin V, was willing to go along with that assertion for the sake of church order. But when the council also called for a regular (or frequent) assembly of bishops to oversee the work of the church, Martin promptly ignored them.

Such disregard did not last, and Martin's papal successor, Eugenius IV, had to fend off his power from bishops who repeated the calls for councils from Constance. The conflict over church power that absorbed much of the hierarchy's attention during the fifteenth century allowed secular authorities to claim more and more control over church life in their jurisdictions. As Brad Gregory writes, "Tired of prelates making the church worse instead of better, significant numbers of secular authorities at every level used their new power to oversee ecclesiastical reforms."[6] What is striking about this admission from a historian who blames the Reformation for setting into motion the worst features of Western society's decadence and relativism is that European secular authorities' grasping for power over the church, whatever it might say about church-state relations, was

---

5. Gregory, *Unintended Reformation*, 142.
6. Gregory, *Unintended Reformation*, 143.

a consequence of the papacy's decadence and self-absorption. The institution that was supposed to represent Christ on earth—the one to guarantee holiness, truth, and unity—had become a cesspool of political intrigue and personal wantonness. To be sure, papal authority never rested on personal holiness. All church officers, Roman Catholic or Protestant, are sinners and are capable of abusing their ecclesiastical authority. Even so, an argument that popes cannot be perfect fails to recognize how much hangs in the balance when the officer who makes Rome superior to every other Christian communion because of his authority and capacity to teach and unite and who gives coherence to Roman Catholicism engages in gross negligence. The failure of the medieval papacy threw into question all the claims of high papalists who argued that the bishop of Rome was the final authority on earth for the church's ministry. If Christians could not trust that bishop, what should they do? The only thing that Roman Catholic historians like Brad Gregory can do is shrug: "Whatever its problems, it was the only church there was, or could be."[7] That affirmation presumes any other church, like a Lutheran or Reformed one, is impossible. It also excuses popes and bishops of any dereliction of duty. If Roman Catholicism is the only possible church, so much for ever reforming that church since Christians are stuck with whoever is in charge.

Gregory also notices that even as Europe's secular authorities began to take church reform into their hands, the papacy, once restored after the Council of Constance, did little to avoid its previous waywardness. In fact, the assertion of secular autonomy from papal control of church life left the papacy without sources of revenue it needed to make Rome the center of the Western church. To rectify the papacy's depleted coffers, Renaissance popes increased the number of venal offices—lords and local rulers in the political territories controlled by the pope (the Papal States). They also turned to the sale of indulgences as another way to raise revenues. Another Roman Catholic historian, Eamon Duffy, asserts that the fifteenth-century

---

7. Gregory, *Unintended Reformation*, 144.

papacy had descended from "the universal pastors of the Church" to "Italian politicians." Another reason for enhancing the status of the papacy was to attract pilgrims to Rome—one part financial, one part devotional—since pilgrims spent money and also desired piously to see relics. To make Rome the center of the Western church and "the greatest of all earthly cities," even "the mother of Europe," the Renaissance popes planned and built streets and palaces "to perpetuate their own and their families' names."[8] In other words, at the very time that the crisis of the papacy should have taught the lesson of church reform, the papacy doubled down on enhancing its own standing and environs. Quite plausible was the conclusion of any observer at the time that merely tinkering with canon law, or making popes accountable to councils, or recruiting holy churchmen for office would have no lasting effect. The papacy appeared to be a corrupt institution in part because episcopacy itself—rule by one—protected bishops from accountability while also tempting them to use their authority to enhance their powers.

Gregory argues that what separated Protestants from earlier efforts at reform was that conciliarists and secular authorities attempted to work within the structures of the church while the Reformers chose to go outside inherited patterns. In one sense, that claim is wrongheaded since the same secular authorities who tried reforms in the fifteenth century were the ones who in the sixteenth century turned to Luther or Calvin to head up the church within their territories. And that occurred only after the papacy and magisterium refused to budge in its way of conducting church affairs. Protestants did not simply start a new denomination. That was impossible in a church-state system in which the government recognized only one church. Only if a state, kingdom, or city gained autonomy from the papacy or emperor could it then start to regulate religious affairs in its own jurisdiction—which is what happened in Luther's Saxony and Calvin's Geneva.

---

8. Duffy, *Saints and Sinners*, 133.

At the same time, Gregory has a point if he means that Reformers like Luther recognized that the teaching of the church on salvation and worship kept the papacy in power and made reform impossible. Rome's teaching on sin and grace set into motion practices, like selling indulgences, that increased the venality of the papacy and its "eternal city." When Protestants began to pick apart Rome's teaching on the gospel, the Reformers also began to pick at the mortar of an ecclesiastical facade that began to crumble. Could Leo X, for instance, have embraced justification by faith alone? He had the power to do so, and no official council had weighed in on justification the way that the Council of Trent eventually did. So a pope could have endorsed Luther's teaching. But the personal and professional incentives for doing so were decidedly with maintaining the status quo—retaining the papacy as the center of Europe's political and cultural life. Somehow, attending to those worldly affairs would also provide adequate spiritual counsel and assistance for sinners in need of a savior.

The Formation of the Papacy

Just as Roman Catholic apologists like to talk about the historical developments that led to the formation of the canon of Scripture, so Protestants can observe that the papacy did not drop down from Christ's ascension. If history leads Roman Catholics to think that the church came before Scripture, history also leads in the direction of recognizing that the formation of the canon of the Bible actually took place before the papacy emerged as the central institution of the Western church. It also shows that the reason for the rise of papal supremacy—the priority of the bishop of Rome over all other bishops—had as much to do with the politics of Europe as it did with anything Jesus said to Peter.

For the first three centuries of church history, when Christianity was not part of the political establishment but on the outside of the Roman Empire looking in—and sometimes persecuted fiercely—the bishop of Rome was nothing like what the office became after the fall of Rome in AD 476. Roman Catholic historians themselves reveal that the earliest "popes" did not emerge directly from the apostle

Peter but started to show vigor only in the second century. At first, presbyters or presbyter-bishops oversaw the Church of Rome. Even when a monarchical bishop did arise, the priority and supremacy of Rome was not self-evident. In the second and third centuries, popes opposed the practices of bishops elsewhere (over the date of Easter and the rebaptism of heretics), but church officials felt no obligation to submit to Rome's authority.

When the Roman Empire in the West began to fray and tear, the pope emerged as Western Europe's lasting tie to the authority and antiquity of Rome. Rather than the bishop of Rome having to reckon with the Christian emperor as bishops in the East did, the papacy was able to craft a policy of church-state relations that made the bishop of Rome the head of ecclesiastical matters and God's representative, in some ways above princes and kings. The weakening of ties between the empire in the East and the Western church, from the sixth century on, also prompted the papacy to establish alliances with European rulers. These diplomatic ties were crucial especially when local Italian forces opposed, obstructed, and engaged in war with the leaders of the city of Rome. The alliance between Pope Leo III and Charlemagne, king of the Franks, became the tie out of which emerged the Holy Roman Empire of Western Europe. In 800, after Charlemagne had traveled to Italy to put down a rebellion against the pope, Leo inaugurated him as the holy emperor of the Romans at the Mass on Christmas day. On the one hand, this arrangement bestowed great power on Charlemagne and gave the West its own version of the first Christian emperor, Constantine. At the same time, the papacy's authority to confer such a title on a secular ruler also implied the bishop of Rome was himself a ruler who could give religious and political unity to European society.

The political intrigue that surrounded the papacy and added to its luster before the eleventh century was no match for the claims to papal supremacy that increased with frequency and fervency during the High Middle Ages. The pope's increased authority originated from genuine efforts to purge the church of corruption. Eamon Duffy observes that by the eleventh century, monasteries and bishoprics were "enormously" wealthy social and political corporations. Secular rulers needed to do business with the church or try to use it to enhance revenue and authority. Duffy adds that the potential for corruption in all this was "obvious," and simony, the buying of church office, was a constant temptation.[9] Beginning with Gregory VII (1073–1085), a series of reforming popes who tried to preserve the church's integrity and autonomy by establishing papal control over explicitly religious affairs held office. Gregory's showdown with King Henry IV in the Investiture Controversy (Does the pope or the emperor invest bishops with authority?) was a sign of the papacy's increased vigor in regulating church affairs. During this period of Gregorian reform, claims for papal supremacy shifted. Rather than asserting that popes were successors of Peter or deputies of the apostle, specific popes and canon lawyers spoke of the papacy as the representatives, or "vicars," of Christ. The pope became Europe's Moses, the lawgiver and judge to whom the church and the rest of society looked as the final authority on religious matters, if not on most of life, because all of life comes from God. Rome, in other words, became the "executive centre of the Church," with the Vatican growing to handle "the increase of business."[10]

Important to notice about this transformation of the papacy was how late the supreme authority of Rome occurred. Some apologists for Roman Catholicism claim that their church was the one Christ founded. But Rome is a long way from Jerusalem, the only diocese that Christ would have experienced in His earthly existence. So too the Rome of high papalism was a long way from the bishops of the second century who had virtually no standing with or access to Rome's political authorities.

Just as important to notice is not simply the historical anachronism of thinking papal supremacy was what Jesus and Peter had in mind but also how rife with corruption a central authority in the church could be. To be sure, placing restrictions on secular

---

9. Duffy, *Saints and Sinners*, 89.
10. Duffy, *Saints and Sinners*, 99.

authorities who sought to use the church for personal or political gain was a valuable aim. But doing so, making the pope the sole sovereign, removed any real check or oversight from the papacy and so merely shifted the potential for corruption from the secular to the religious sphere. In fact, theologians in the thirteenth century, as Francis Oakley meticulously shows, developed a theory of papal supremacy that made it virtually impossible for Roman Catholicism to walk back from papal sovereignty in any form. The terms used to describe the pope captured the investment that theologians and church officials were placing in the bishop of Rome: "Successor of Peter, Vicar of Christ, Roman pontiff, 'primate and patriarch,' 'universal shepherd and ruler,' 'supreme hierarch and monarch of the whole Church Militant,' the pope is not simply king but 'king of kings.'" The pope has this power directly from Christ, according to the theologians writing almost thirteen centuries after Christ uttered the words recorded in Matthew's gospel to Peter. Not only was this supreme sovereign the legitimate ruler over all churches in the spiritual realm but he was also over all civil authorities. As such, "the pope had full judgment over all princes and according to every mode of judgment that has been communicated to the spiritual power."[11]

Such an assertion of authority in one office—one that was often a political toy fought over by Rome's elite families—made ecclesiastical reform a tough sell. Since every ruler in Europe was a Christian and subject of the church, and since all bishops and priests received their authority only in ordination through the papacy, finding a legitimate authority to challenge the pope when he sinned or erred was as difficult as Englishmen, Frenchmen, or Scots looking for ways to challenge divine-right monarchs who based their power on a divine commission. As some thirteenth-century theologians also noted, rule by one was the best form of government when you had a good and wise king. But monarchy readily turned into tyranny and the worst form of government if the king was wicked. Beginning in the fourteenth and

---

11. Francis Oakley, *The Mortgage of the Past: Reshaping the Ancient Political Inheritance (1050–1300)* (New Haven, Conn.: Yale University Press, 2012), 134, 135.

fifteenth centuries, Europeans began to look for alternatives to monarchy, such as republics, because of the abuses of princes and kings. The Reformation was part of the same process when the Reformers began to look for alternatives to the papacy for governing the church. Rather than proving the legitimacy and superiority of Roman Catholicism, the papacy actually was responsible for the crisis of authority in late medieval Europe. To the Reformers' credit, they also recognized, due to abuses of worship and doctrine, that much of the system of salvation available in the Western church only added to the pope's control. If church reform was going to happen, and many throughout the church recognized the need, it would require more than regular meetings of bishops. It would need a reform of the church in doctrine, worship, and government.

Papal Supremacy Alive and Ticking

The dogma of papal infallibility did not become official until the First Vatican Council of 1870. This doctrine of infallibility became the formal teaching of the church at a time when the papacy was part of a serious political crisis in Italy. Throughout most of its history, the papacy had regularly depended on European powers to defend itself from foreign and Italian invaders who wanted to rule in Rome. Even with his own military, the pope was not strong enough to protect the Papal States. Indeed, one of the reasons for crowning Charlemagne the Holy Roman emperor was payback to the Frankish king for protecting the pope. By the nineteenth century, however, the papacy's function as a civil ruler looked increasingly anomalous and for Italians was a major barrier to a unified nation. Germany was in the last stages of efforts to unify itself as a nation under Bismarck, and the United States had recently conducted a civil war to maintain "the union." The logic of nineteenth-century statecraft was administrative centralization. But the papacy and its territory were in the way of Italian unification. In 1871, Italy finally achieved national unity, and the Papal States became part of the new nation. Was it coincidental that the papacy, having lost its temporal power, raised the stakes of its spiritual power by making papal infallibility a dogma? Whatever the answer, the doctrine of papal infallibility was just one more instance of the papacy's domination of Roman Catholic life and its conservative posture between the Council of Trent and the Second Vatican Council. As Pius IX, the same pope to formalize infallibility, taught in the infamous Syllabus of Errors (1864), the idea that the pope "can, and ought to, reconcile himself, and come to terms with progress, liberalism and modern civilization" was false. As the rest of the world became modern (for good and ill) after the Reformation, the papacy held on to its medieval identity.

The Second Vatican Council, then, represented an effort to move the church into the modern world and to bring, as the conciliarists of the fifteenth century wanted, the pope and the bishops into a more reciprocal relationship. In the dogmatic constitution of the Council, *Lumen Gentium*, the bishops walked a fine line between respecting papal authority and recognizing the legitimate status of bishops and councils. The word they chose instead of *council* was *college*, as in "St. Peter and the other apostles constitute one apostolic college, so in a similar way the Roman Pontiff, the successor of Peter, and the bishops, the successors of the apostles, are joined together" (para. 22). How the pope and bishops related was complicated:

> The Roman Pontiff, as the successor of Peter, is the perpetual and visible principle and foundation of unity of both the bishops and of the faithful. The individual bishops, however, are the visible principle and foundation of unity in their particular churches, fashioned after the model of the universal Church, in and from which churches comes into being the one and only Catholic Church. For this reason the individual bishops represent each his own church, but all of them together and with the Pope represent the entire Church in the bond of peace, love and unity. (para. 23)

At the same time, *Lumen Gentium* prevented bishops from gaining autonomy: "The college or body of bishops has no authority unless it is understood together with the Roman Pontiff" (para. 23). Even so, as John O'Malley argues, collegiality prevailed at the council due to an effort to recover earlier sources of Christian faith and practice.

For many bishops, the council was tapping ways that the church had governed itself (as Protestants have long argued) before the eleventh century, when papal primacy "virtually pushed" the cooperation of bishops "off the ecclesiastical map."[12] In effect, the argument that the church had for its first one thousand years functioned collegially— without papal supremacy, as Roman Catholic apologists tirelessly argue—prevailed at the Second Vatican Council, which means that some apologists who love papal supremacy do not pay attention to or defer to the official teachings of the bishops, including the pope, they so aggressively defend.

And yet the reforms of the Second Vatican Council and the implicit recognition of the Reformers' objections to papal supremacy have not saved Rome from the dangers of episcopal governance and bureaucratic red tape. Reporters who cover the Vatican regularly write stories about Pope Francis as a reformer who is trying to implement changes in the way the Vatican operates. Among those reforms are making the Vatican bank more transparent, a new communications effort, and consolidation of diverse offices for efficiency's sake. Plus, the pope has tried to govern in a much more collegial way by relying on a Council of Cardinals (nine prelates) and sponsoring synods of bishops to oversee aspects of church life, family and marriage most recently. But Francis's reforms have proved to be ineffective if only because the church and its administrative apparatus are so big. As John Allen recently wrote: "The Catholic Church is a 1.2-billion strong family of faith present in every nook and cranny of the planet, and it's perpetually in danger of spinning apart, fragmenting into thousands of disparate local churches.... Somebody has to codify the teaching, promulgate the laws, develop the policies and issue the guidelines to hold such a far-flung global community together, and obviously no pope can do that all by himself."[13] This means having a large Roman Curia that is necessary for doing all the administration

---

12. O'Malley, *Trent: What Happened at the Council*, 302.

13. John L. Allen Jr., "The Risks of Pope Francis's Never-Ending Vatican Reform," Crux, December 22, 2016, https://cruxnow.com/analysis/2016/12/22/risks -pope-franciss-never-ending-vatican-reform/.

required for a centralized international organization (like the United Nations) and that is so set in its ways that reform, even by a pope, is next to impossible.

The underside of this bureaucratic behemoth is a history of hiding behind spiritual authority when scandals hit Roman Catholicism. The most recent that rocked church members, especially in the United States, was the revelation of priests in the archdiocese of Boston who had sexually abused children. As the Notre Dame historian John McGreevy astutely observes, the instances of sexual abuse, as wicked as they were, especially from men who had taken vows of obedience and chastity, were arguably "no worse" than Boy Scout leaders, public school teachers, or Protestant pastors who, according to statistics, were as guilty of pedophilia as priests. The real scandal for the Roman Catholic Church, then, was not the sinfulness of priests but the extent to which bishops and cardinals covered up such behavior. McGreevy observes that disclosure of "secret diocesan settlements highlighted the absence of adequate financial controls... and the need for lay Catholic oversight of personnel issues." That became even more apparent after the public learned that the three most influential cardinals in the American church—Bernard Law in Boston, Edward Egan in New York, and Roger Mahoney in Los Angeles—had handled their cases of wayward priests "callously."[14] For anyone to expect church officials to be sinless and operate without any mistakes or misjudgments is folly. But for bishops who claim to be descendants of the apostles and who have throughout the history of Christianity pulled rank as the surest way to protect the truth of Christianity and shepherd the faithful to use their power to cover up for gross instances of immorality is its own form of nonsense.

Indeed, the priest sex scandal is simply the latest high profile instance of the flaws inherent in episcopal forms of church government. Because church officers are sinners, they need checks and balances, just like those that Americans celebrate in the U.S.

---

14. John T. McGreevy, *Catholicism and American Freedom: A History* (New York: W. W. Norton, 2004), 291.

Constitution. But the papacy and the system of episcopacy that it has shepherded for the last millennium have not allowed real forms of peer review and internal oversight to emerge. How could Roman Catholicism ever submit its bishops to some kind of lay oversight when the entire point of having bishops is to pass on faithfully and flawlessly the teachings and ministry of Christ and the apostles?

That situation leaves Roman Catholicism just as broken as it was in the days of Martin Luther. McGreevy notes that Roman Catholicism is caught in a set of polarities. It is on the one hand the largest Christian communion in the world and enrolls "more active members than any other in American society." On the other hand, it is "a wounded, fractious church, ripped apart by disputes over sex, gender, and ministry, and incapable of sustaining the loyalty of many of its communicants."[15] Protestantism may not be able to claim the size, influence, history, or administrative heft of Roman Catholicism. But people who grow up Protestant and convert to Roman Catholicism, thinking they have arrived at the true and unified church, are severely mistaken. The same sorts of problems that beset the Roman Church for two centuries before the Reformation have not gone away. Roman Catholicism still needs its system of church government reformed. One place to start, as the Reformers understood, was with the papacy. But reducing the role of the papacy is next to impossible because without the bishop of Rome, Catholicism would not be Roman. And without Rome, Catholicism would lose most of its luster.

---

15. McGreevy, *Catholicism and American Freedom*, 293.

5

VOCATION: SPIRITUALITY FOR ORDINARY LIFE

If twentieth-century Protestants associated the phrase "full-time Christian service" with fundamentalism, they forgot an important lesson of the Reformation. Ironically, Protestant children who grew up aspiring to live lives devoted to evangelism, missions, or the ministry because these were the occupations in which someone could serve God 24/7 were not that far removed from an outlook that Protestantism challenged and replaced. Before the Reformation, Western Christianity gave believers little instruction on how to serve God in so-called secular activities like work outside the church—in the field, in the mine, in the home, in the marketplace, or in city council. Eamon Duffy, author of the highly regarded and somewhat nostalgic study of medieval piety *The Stripping of the Altars*, makes this point implicitly by arguing that the church set the agenda for the laity and how they made sense of their activities in the world. He opens his book with this observation: "Within that great seasonal cycle of fast and festival, of ritual observance and symbolic gesture, lay Christians found the paradigms and the stories which shaped their perception of the world and their place in it." In the liturgy and church calendar, Duffy adds, "medieval people found the key to the meaning and purpose of their lives."[1]

For those seeking justification for Roman Catholicism and its comprehensive outlook, Duffy's account is consoling, but for

---

1. Eamon Duffy, *The Stripping of the Altars: Traditional Religion in England, c. 1400–c. 1580* (New Haven, Conn.: Yale University Press, 1992), 11.

Christians who hoped to live holy lives in their activities away from church, the ministry of Roman Catholicism was sparse. If a farmer or a miner or a knight wanted to serve God in his occupation, the church offered no instruction and little encouragement. In fact, the model of monasticism and the ideals of the priestly life—vows of celibacy, poverty, and obedience to superiors—were the chief outlets for Roman Catholics wanting to live a life devoted to God. For instance, Benedict, the founder of the Benedictine monastery, opened his rule with this explanation:

> And so we are going to establish a school for the service of the Lord. In founding it we hope to introduce nothing harsh or burdensome. But if a certain strictness results from the dictates of equity for the amendment of vices or the preservation of charity, do not be at once dismayed and fly from the way of salvation, whose entrance cannot but be narrow (Matt. 7:14). For as we advance in the religious life and in faith, our hearts expand and we run the way of God's commandments with unspeakable sweetness of love.[2]

Becoming a monk was the way to pursue salvation. The problem was, you needed to go to the monastery to pursue a life of holiness. In other words, you needed to be in full-time Christian service to pursue a life ultimately pleasing to God. If you were not a monk, nun, priest, or bishop, the path of salvation was murky at best.

The chief outlets for laypeople seeking to live a godly life, aside from observance of the Mass, which the laity received only once a year typically despite its frequent performance by priests and monks, were prayer and pilgrimage. One of the chief outlets for prayer was the Mass. Over time the sacrament became less a means for the laity to partake of Christ's body and blood and more an opportunity to pray for the dead. Churches increasingly saw the proliferation of altars within cathedrals and basilicas so that priests could say many Masses that would assist the departed to leave purgatory and arrive

---

2. Prologue to *Saint Benedict's Rule for Monasteries*, trans. Leonard J. Doyle (Collegeville, Minn.: Order of St. Benedict, 2001), http://www.osb.org/rb/text/toc .html#toc.

in heaven. Related to this system of assisting the deceased was the notion of a treasury of merits, in which good works performed in this life might be transferred to those in purgatory who were deficient. Being charitable—giving alms to assist the poor, support hospitals, or contribute to the construction of buildings or bridges—was a way that laity could work out their own salvation and aid those who had died. Preparing for death, consequently, was a major part of lay piety, and it featured grace-assisted works that would give believers a better chance on judgment day.

Some laity left the world of secular work to become monks or nuns. Monasticism exemplified the fundamental divide between the holy and the profane in a person's quest for salvation. Prior to the twelfth century, monasticism had been the way for an ordinary man to pursue a holy life, but the need for more clergy to say the Mass for the living and the dead created a demand that monks be ordained as priests. At roughly the same time in the twelfth century, the requirement of monastic celibacy migrated from the monastery to all priests. The rise of confraternities was one way to accommodate the appeal of monasticism for laypeople. These were voluntary organizations that bound their members by vows and allowed the laity to live in the secular world while also having direct ties to a group of similarly committed Christians. Although prayer was an important part of these confraternities, they also contributed to works of mercy and penitence. Some confraternities performed charitable activities in communities and so contributed to the treasury of merits for those involved. Others were explicitly penitential in character, and repentance took the form of punishing the flesh, or self-flagellation. According to André Vauchez, confraternities of penitents and flagellants "were clearly animated by the desire to appropriate the spiritual resources of monasticism." He adds that the laity "aspired to escape from their subordinate position in religious life" and so borrowed from the model of monks.[3] The overall effect of Roman Catholic

---

3. André Vauchez, *The Laity in the Middle Ages: Religious Beliefs and Devotional Practices* (South Bend, Ind.: University of Notre Dame Press, 1996), 114.

piety was to provide a two-tiered system, with those in the holy orders (clergy and monks) at the top and the laity toward the bottom, looking up. For laypeople, the most obvious way to be devout was to imitate those who had given their lives over to full-time Christian service.

Protestantism offered a remarkable alternative to this system of piety. As important as reforms in doctrine, worship, and church government were, they did not necessarily trickle down to the ordinary lives of laypeople who needed to labor at jobs, feed children, change diapers, herd sheep, and clean homes. Justification by faith alone was a marvelous relief to the threat of sin's consequences and ground for good works. Worship disciplined by God's Word was amazingly accessible for people who had gone to church often to "watch" the service. And oversight by pastors and elders provided encouragement and direction to average Christians. But these reforms did not necessarily resolve the tension between holy or religious activities—such as word, sacraments, and prayer—and common duties and practices like work, eating, and play. The Protestant doctrine of vocation, the idea that ordinary believers serve God and love their neighbor in regular activities, was a breakthrough for the laity. The Reformation not only changed church life but also transformed secular society by elevating the so-called secular world to a place where Christians could be as devout in their "worldly employments and recreations" as pastors and theologians.

The Spiritual Estate of All Believers

In one of his most important early essays, "An Open Letter to the Christian Nobility of the German Nation," Luther made a claim that in 1520 was unthinkable. He appealed to the princes of the German-speaking territories to disregard papal authority and take the lead in carrying out reform in the churches in their lands. Luther did this by invoking the Protestant doctrine so popular that it qualifies as a bumper-sticker truth: the priesthood of all believers. Luther objected to church teaching that categorized Christians according to spiritual estates—the clergy and a temporal estate, people who worked in the secular world. All Christians, he wrote, "are truly of the 'spiritual estate,'" such that the only difference was one of office. "We are all one body," he added, "yet every member has its own work, where by it serves every other, all because we have one baptism, one Gospel, one faith, and are all alike Christians."[4] What made Christians spiritual was not ordination but baptism, the gospel, and faith alone.

To be sure, this argument played directly to Luther's advantage, but it would also have implications for Christian life well beyond his situation. In the give-and-take of his controversy with Leo X, Luther faced the high hurdle of papal supremacy. How could he challenge the head of the church with support merely from his own prince, Frederick III of Saxony? By the logic of medieval theology, princes had temporal power but not spiritual authority. But if Luther could invest secular authorities with spiritual power by virtue of the doctrine of the priesthood of all believers, he might conceivably challenge papal sovereignty with a legitimate rival spiritual power. Even so, Luther's assertion of unqualified priesthood applied well beyond the specific politics of Germany's relationship to the papacy. For Luther, every Christian possessed a calling or vocation that was part of their spiritual service to God and neighbor. "Those who are now called 'spiritual'—priests, bishops or popes," Luther wrote, "are neither different from other Christians nor superior to them, except that they are charged with the administration of the Word of God and the sacraments, which is their work and office." Likewise, "temporal authorities" have the responsibility to "punish the evil and to protect the good." But Luther did not stop with the work of the church or the state. "A cobbler, a smith, a farmer, each has the work and office of his trade, and yet they are all alike consecrated priests and bishops."[5]

Luther's logic did not stem from an anticlericalism that insisted every person was competent to minister God's word or from an egalitarianism that hoped for the elimination of all hierarchical distinctions. Instead, the Reformer held to a different understanding of the church from the dominant one that divided the people of God

---

4. Luther, "Open Letter to the Christian Nobility," 66.
5. Luther, "Open Letter to the Christian Nobility," 69.

into spiritual and secular spheres. He argued that everyone who belonged to the body of Christ was called to serve the entire body, as Paul taught about spiritual gifts in 1 Corinthians 11 and Romans 12. Luther echoed the apostle when he wrote, "Every one by means of his own work or office must benefit and serve every other." Whether someone's responsibility was to minister word and sacrament or to make shoes or bake bread, these tasks were to be "done for the bodily and spiritual welfare of the community." But the existing distinctions between the sacred and the secular, between the holy life of monks and clergy and the worldly lives of knights and peasants, segregated Christians into airtight departments and elevated spiritual work above activities outside the church or monastery. That hierarchy also involved the understanding that those in secular activities, like magistrates, could not reform the church since the spiritual functions of ministry were above the prince's pay grade. Luther thought this understanding of the church bordered on nonsense. If Christian magistrates could not involve themselves in the affairs of the church, then "the tailors, cobblers, masons, carpenters, pot-boys, tapsters, farmers, and all the secular tradesmen, should also be prevented from providing pope, bishops, priests and monks with shoes, clothing, houses, meat and drink, and from paying them tribute."[6] The New Testament's teaching on the church as the body of Christ, with each member possessing unique responsibilities that contributed to the health and well-being of the body, was at the root of Luther's notion of vocation. Because all Christians served the wider body in their occupations, their work was spiritual service, priestly in character.

John Calvin shared Luther's understanding of vocation and bolstered it with his own exegesis of important scriptural texts, such as the gospel narrative of Jesus's visit to Mary and Martha, a text often used to support the Roman Catholic position that the contemplative life of Mary, who sat at Jesus's feet, was superior to the active life of Martha, the one doing so much work she became exasperated with her sister:

---

6. Luther, "Open Letter to the Christian Nobility," 69, 70.

> But Martha was distracted with much serving, and she approached Him and said, "Lord, do you not care that my sister has left me to serve alone? Tell her then to help me."
>
> And Jesus answered and said to her, "Martha, Martha, you are worried and troubled about many things. But one thing is needed, and Mary has chosen that good part, which will not be taken away from her." (Luke 10:40–42)

According to Thomas Aquinas, Christ's aim in this story was to teach that "the contemplative life is more excellent than the active."[7]

But in his commentary on the Gospels, Calvin rejected the standard medieval interpretation. He did not deny that Christ recommended Mary over Martha. But Jesus's endorsement of Mary was not a blanket approval of the spiritual life over the rough and tumble of domestic or earthly chores. Calvin observed:

> How absurdly they have perverted the words of Christ to support their own contrivance, will appear manifest when we have ascertained the natural meaning. Luke says that Mary sat at the feet of Jesus. Does he mean that she did nothing else throughout her whole life? On the contrary, the Lord enjoins his followers to make such a distribution of their time, that he who desires to make proficiency in the school of Christ shall not always be an idle hearer but shall put in practice what he has learned; for there is a time to hear, and a time to act. It is, therefore, a foolish attempt of the monks to take hold of this passage, as if Christ were drawing a comparison between a contemplative and an active life, while Christ simply informs us for what end, and in what manner, he wishes to be received.[8]

Calvin added that Martha's fault was not worldly activities instead of religious devotion but failing to keep work within proper bounds. "Christ would rather have chosen to be entertained in a frugal

---

7. Lee Hardy, *The Fabric of This World: Inquiries Into Calling, Career Choice, and the Design of Human Work* (Grand Rapids: Eerdmans, 1990), 55.

8. John Calvin, *Commentary on a Harmony of the Evangelists, Matthew, Mark, and Luke*, trans. William Pringle (repr., Grand Rapids: Baker, 1981), 2:143 (commentary on Luke 10:38–42).

manner," he explained, "and at moderate expense, than that the holy woman should have submitted to so much toil." Martha also failed to notice what was truly important—namely, that Christ Himself was present with her. "It was just as if one were to give a magnificent reception to a prophet, and yet not to care about hearing him, but, on the contrary, to make so great and unnecessary preparations as to bury all the instruction."[9] In other words, the particular circumstance of the incident was the point of the story, not a general recommendation of the spiritual over the secular.

When Calvin discussed the doctrine of vocation in his *Institutes of the Christian Religion*, he approached it in the context of the right use of worldly things or, as he called them, "earthly blessings." He started with an affirmation of the goodness of creation and the necessity of relying on worldly things as long as people lived in this world. Calvin wrote, "If we are to live, we must use the necessary supports of life; nor can we even shun those things which seem more subservient to delight than to necessity." Some of the most basic features of human existence, even a diet of bread and water, went beyond mere necessity to pleasure since a cold cup of water or a warm piece of bread can in certain circumstances bring as much delight as the most expensive meal at the finest restaurant. Here Calvin was well aware of Roman Catholicism's tendency to elevate fasting and abstemiousness as the surest way to holiness. To avoid "luxury and excess," advocates of monasticism, for instance, sought to correct potential sinfulness by counseling austere use of earthly goods. But this was dangerous and had bound consciences of Christians, both clergy and laity, with rules more narrow "than those in which they are bound by the word of God." Indeed, Protestantism offered believers freedom from a kind of monastic piety that prescribed all sorts of regulations that the Bible did not require. Some even went as far as total abstinence, Calvin lamented, by making it "scarcely lawful to make any addition" to a

---

9. Calvin, *Commentary on a Harmony of the Evangelists*, 143, 144 (commentary on Luke 10:38–42).

regimen of bread and water.[10] The biblical teaching about human life was to use the good gifts of creation for "the end for which their author made and destined them," since God created these things "for our good, and not for our destruction." To illustrate the general guideline, which prevented hard and fast rules, Calvin used the example of food and clothing: "If we consider for what end he created food, we shall find that he consulted not only for our necessity, but also for our enjoyment and delight. Thus, in clothing, the end was, in addition to necessity, comeliness and honour; and in herbs, fruits, and trees, besides their various uses, gracefulness of appearance and sweetness of smell. Were it not so, the Prophet would not enumerate among the mercies of God 'wine that maketh glad the heart of man, and oil to make his face to shine' (Ps. 104:15)."[11]

This was the same framework within which Calvin considered a Christian's occupation in this life: What was the end, or purpose, of work since a person could not avoid some form of employment and since Scripture forbade laziness and indolence? He used the word "calling" to refer to the "actions in life" that God had assigned to every person. These callings performed a negative function—to keep Christians from "restlessness of the human mind," "fickleness," and "ambition." Each person possessed from God's providential design "distinct duties" in "different modes of life." For that reason, the doctrine of vocation was a general notion that applied in a broad way to all lawful employments (one could not be called to be a thief or prostitute).

And yet the constraints of vocation were ultimately positive in effect: "Every man's mode of life, therefore, is a kind of station assigned him by the Lord, that he may not be always driven about at random." Vocation gave a person direction and purpose. It yielded a form of relief from having continually to decide what to do with life. The circumstances of providing for a family, the kind of work available, the

---

10. John Calvin, *Institutes of the Christian Religion*, trans. Henry Beveridge (Edinburgh: Calvin Translation Society, 1845–1846), 3.10.1, http://www.ccel.org/ccel/calvin/institutes.i.html.

11. Calvin, *Institutes*, 3.10.2.

idiosyncrasies of employers, the laws governing a particular society—all these aspects of work placed limits on a person so that he or she could do something productive and avoid activities harmful or even sinful. "Every one in his particular mode of life will, without repining, suffer its inconveniences, cares, uneasiness, and anxiety, persuaded that God has laid on the burden," Calvin concluded. "This, too, will afford admirable consolation, that in following your proper calling, no work will be so mean and sordid as not to have a splendour and value in the eye of God."[12] This understanding of work as consolation was a long way from the kind of relief and purpose that had been available only to priests or monks. Now Christians in secular occupations were living as directly before the face of God as the most celibate, poor, and obedient monk.

At the same time, this understanding of vocation was a long way from the Protestant work ethic that the German sociologist Max Weber assigned to Calvinism. According to historian Robert Mitchell, for Calvinists the doctrine of predestination nurtured an outlook on work that compensated for religious doubt:

> The doctrine of predestination, which was the most character-istic dogma of Calvinism, with its inhuman stress on election to salvation, placed man in a place of unprecedented inner loneli-ness before God. No one could help him. No priest or sacrament could bridge the gulf between God and man. The individual was forced to follow his path alone to be the destiny that had already been decreed for him from eternity.... To know how a per-son could be certain that he was one of the elect...one should achieve self-confidence by intense worldly activity.[13]

For all the problems with this analysis, especially the idea that Calvinists were most responsible for economic productivity in early

---

12. Calvin, *Institutes*, 3.10.6.

13. Robert Mitchell, "The Weber Thesis, Pro and Con," *Fides et Historia* 4, no. 2 (1972): 56–57, quoted in R. Scott Clark, "Weber, Election, Capitalism, and Betsy DeVos," *Heidelblog*, January 18, 2017, https://heidelblog.net/2017/01/weber-election-capitalism-and-betsy-devos/.

modern Europe when the proliferation of markets involved much more than Christian doctrine, Weber confused and conflated two different topics—namely, assurance and vocation. Calvinists took comfort for salvation not from their work or economic well-being, as if they were forerunners of gospel-of-prosperity believers. The Heidelberg Catechism could not be clearer about the real source of the believer's confidence. A Christian's only comfort is

> that I, with body and soul, both in life and in death, am not my own, but belong to my faithful Savior Jesus Christ, who with His precious blood has fully satisfied for all my sins, and redeemed me from all the power of the devil; and so preserves me, that without the will of my Father in heaven not a hair can fall from my head; indeed, that all things must work together for my salvation. Wherefore, by His Holy Spirit, He also assures me of eternal life, and makes me heartily willing and ready from now on to live for Him. (Q&A 1)

In health or illness, prosperity or poverty, work or unemployment, a Christian's standing before God, as Protestants taught, depended solely on the righteousness of Christ imputed to the believer through faith alone, by grace alone.

In contrast, one's vocation and work were not part of God's redemptive plan but instead pieces of His providential care for creation. A farmer who milks cows is exhibiting God's care for part of His creation. A butcher who sells meat to neighbors is participating in God's provision for His creation. A man who provides for his wife and children is exhibiting part of God's providential care for His people. Work, in other words, while done to the glory of God, makes the greatest difference in its effects on this world. Luther captured this insight in his reflections on marriage. The responsibilities of that vocation were large and some were unpleasant, as Luther conceded:

> Now observe that when that clever harlot, our natural reason (which the pagans followed in trying to be most clever), takes a look at married life, she turns up her nose and says, "Alas, must I rock the baby, wash its diapers, make its bed, smell its stench, stay up nights with it, take care of it when it cries, heal its rashes

and sores, and on top of that care for my wife, provide for her, labour at my trade, take care of this and take care of that, do this and do that, endure this and endure that, and whatever else of bitterness and drudgery married life involves?... It is better to remain free and lead a peaceful, carefree life; I will become a priest or a nun and compel my children to do likewise."[14]

How should a believer respond?

O God, because I am certain that thou hast created me as a man and hast from my body begotten this child, I also know for a certainty that it meets with thy perfect pleasure. I confess to thee that I am not worthy to rock the little babe or wash its diapers or to be entrusted with the care of the child and its mother. How is it that I, without any merit, have come to this distinction of being certain that I am serving thy creature and thy most precious will? O how gladly will I do so, though the duties should be even more insignificant and despised. Neither frost nor heat, neither drudgery nor labour, will distress or dissuade me, for I am certain that it is thus pleasing in thy sight.[15]

Luther added that a wife who "suckles the child, rocks and bathes it, and cares for it in other ways" performs "truly golden and noble works."

That was the insight of the Protestant recovery of the doctrine of vocation. It was not a way to enjoy a better life, become a success, or make money. It was recognition of the interconnectedness of creation and the way that God used even tasks considered secular or worldly to sustain His creation. What Protestants did was to give a rationale for the legitimacy of such labor. It was not sacred, but it was still godly. As such, it was as commendable as any explicitly religious activity like preaching, evangelism, or missions.

---

14. Martin Luther, quoted in Gene Veith, "Luther on Changing a Baby's Diaper (Rerun)," *Cranach* (blog), September 15, 2014, http://www.patheos.com/blogs/geneveith/2014/09/luther-on-changing-a-babys-diaper-rerun/.

15. Luther, quoted in Veith, "Luther on Changing," http://www.patheos.com/blogs/geneveith/2014/09/luther-on-changing-a-babys-diaper-rerun/.

Rome Learns from Wittenberg and Geneva

The church hierarchy's response to Luther's and Calvin's ideas about vocation was mixed. On the one hand, the Council of Trent explicitly condemned (anathematized) the doctrine of the priesthood of believers, the bedrock of the Protestant teaching about the service of laypeople in their ordinary work: "If any one affirm, that all Christians indiscriminately are priests of the New Testament, or that they are all mutually endowed with an equal spiritual power, he clearly does nothing but confound the ecclesiastical hierarchy, which is as an army set in array; as if, contrary to the doctrine of blessed Paul, all were apostles, all prophets, all evangelists, all pastors, all doctors" (Seventh Session, ch. 4).

On the other hand, two years into the Council of Trent in 1548, Pope Paul III approved a text written two decades earlier by Ignatius of Loyola, the founder of the Society of Jesus, whose members are called Jesuits and are sometimes referred to as the shock troops of the Counter-Reformation because of their educational efforts, which posed an alternative to the schools and literacy promoted by Protestantism. Ignatius's *Spiritual Exercises* provided a manual in devotional training that the Jesuits used for induction into the Society but that over time also became a vehicle for the laity to pursue a life devoted to Christ.

What is striking about the *Spiritual Exercises* is that they perpetuate the older Roman Catholic model of the contemplative life. By meditation and prayer conducted in retreat from worldly or secular occupations, a Christian deepens his or her faith. What Christians do in their activities, in the ordinary duties of work and family life, is something that Ignatius failed to consider. For example, Ignatius proposed a series of routines for increasing holiness. One was a system of self-examination, three times a day at regularly appointed times, to guard against any particular sin or defect. He also proposed a method for examining thoughts that might encourage mortal sin. The exercises themselves were four sets of plans for prayers to avoid sin, with additional instruction for avoiding pleasurable thoughts, laughter, or even light while undergoing these prayers. In other words, Ignatius's system required its adherents to relinquish most thoughts about worldly activities and duties. It was a plan of spiritual disciplines that were entirely removed from the workaday world for laity who used it as a way of following monastic discipline without entering a monastery.

Only with the Second Vatican Council did church hierarchy finally affirm the laity and their work in ways that Protestants had four centuries earlier. In the council's Decree on the Apostolate of the Laity (*Apostolicam Actuositatem*), the bishops went well beyond Luther's assertion of the priesthood of all believers. They affirmed the apostolic character of the laity:

> Christ conferred on the Apostles and their successors the duty of teaching, sanctifying, and ruling in His name and power. But the laity likewise share in the priestly, prophetic, and royal office of Christ and therefore have their own share in the mission of the whole people of God in the Church and in the world.
>
> They exercise the apostolate in fact by their activity directed to the evangelization and sanctification of men and to the penetrating and perfecting of the temporal order through the spirit of the Gospel. In this way, their temporal activity openly bears witness to Christ and promotes the salvation of men. Since the laity, in accordance with their state of life, live in the midst of the world and its concerns, they are called by God to exercise their apostolate in the world like leaven, with the ardor of the spirit of Christ.[16]

Likewise, in the Dogmatic Constitution of the Church (*Lumen Gentium*), the council affirmed the value of worldly labors in ways that echoed Luther and Calvin. The laity, "by their competence in secular training and by their activity, elevated from within by the grace of Christ," should "vigorously contribute their effort, so that created goods may be perfected by human labor, technical skill and civic cul-

---

16. *Apostolicam Actuositatem*, Documents of the Second Vatican Council, The Holy See, http://www.vatican.va/archive/hist_councils/ii_vatican_council/documents/vat-ii_decree_19651118_apostolicam-actuositatem_en.html.

ture for the benefit of all men according to the design of the Creator and the light of His Word." In so doing, "through the members of the Church, will Christ progressively illumine the whole of human society with His saving light."[17]

And just as the priesthood of all believers asserted by Luther and elaborated in Calvin's doctrine of vocation had eliminated the rationale for entering monasteries (not to mention the appeal of ecclesiastical property to kings and princes looking for revenue), so the Second Vatican Council's affirmation of the laity undercut the church's dependence on and rationale for the religious (monks and nuns). Indeed, the decline in Roman Catholics pursuing holy orders has been dramatic. One Roman Catholic apologist's estimate is stark:

> The religious orders will soon be virtually non-existent in the United States. For example, in 1965 there were 5,277 Jesuit priests and 3,559 seminarians; in 2000 there were 3,172 priests and 38 seminarians. There were 2,534 OFM Franciscan priests and 2,251 seminarians in 1965; in 2000 there were 1,492 priests and 60 seminarians. There were 2,434 Christian Brothers in 1965 and 912 seminarians; in 2000 there were 959 Brothers and 7 seminarians. There were 1,148 Redemptorist priests in 1965 and 1,128 seminarians; in 2000 there were 349 priests and 24 seminarians. Every major religious order in the United States mirrors these statistics.[18]

The doctrine of justification by faith alone makes a serious difference for the Christian life. It leads to an ordinary life of work and family duties that is not inferior but the appropriate way of honoring God and loving neighbor. It also undermines the need to leave the

---

17. *Lumen Gentium*, Documents of the Second Vatican Council, The Holy See, http://www.vatican.va/archive/hist_councils/ii_vatican_council/documents/vat-ii _const_19641121_lumen-gentium_en.html.

18. Michael Davies, "Appendix 2, Part B: Stark Statistics," in *Liturgical Time Bombs: The Destruction of Catholic Faith through Changes in Catholic Worship* (Charlotte, N.C.: TAN Books, 2013; Catholic Tradition), http://www.catholictradition.org /Eucharist/v2-bombs14b.htm.

world to pursue a life of salvation. Protestants understood this at the time of the Reformation. Roman Catholics have begun to affirm the value of secular work but have not integrated their spiritual demands for salvation with their teaching on the value of worldly vocations.

6

IS PROTESTANTISM NEW?

Roman Catholic apologist Fritz Tuttle writes, "The Catholic Church is the only church that can claim to have been founded by Christ personally. Every other church traces its lineage back to a mere human person such as Martin Luther or John Wesley. The Catholic Church can trace its lineage back to Jesus Christ who appointed St. Peter as the first pope. This line of popes has continued unbroken for almost 2,000 years."[1] The implied claim in this assertion that Roman Catholicism is older than Protestantism is patently true. Martin Luther did not post the Ninety-Five Theses until 1517. John Calvin did not convert to Protestantism until 1534. The Reformed churches of France did not arrive at their first confession of faith until 1559. In every case imaginable, Roman Catholicism became the established version and functioned as the sole legitimate expression of Christianity in the West (i.e., Europe).

But simply being older does not make Roman Catholicism true. If we followed that logic, even in the history of redemption, it leads to some odd conclusions. Moses is older than David. So does that mean Christ's lineage from Israel's great king is less authentic because David is more recent than the man who received the Ten Commandments and was on the ground floor of making the Israelites a nation? Israel is older than the church. Does that mean that modern-day believers should follow the practices of Old Testament Israel in worshiping

---

1. Fritz Tuttle, "Jesus Christ Established a Visible Church on Earth," EWTN Global Catholic Network, http://www.ewtn.com/FAITH/TEACHINGS/churb1.htm.

and serving God? Or that Christianity, because it is new compared to Judaism, is less authentic? Even in the New Testament, the idea of the older the better, the more ancient the more authentic, is prone to paint you into an intellectual corner. Paul comes after Jesus. Does that mean Paul is less authoritative than Jesus when it comes to the inspired and infallible writings for which the apostle was responsible? In other words, if what is older is better and truer, then we have the problem of the higher critics who argued that Paul was the second founder of Christianity. But if Christ sent His Spirit to inspire Paul's writings, then Paul should be as authentic as Jesus or as the authors of the Gospels. Simply saying that something is older does not settle the argument.

Even more important, though, is the crudity and misleading character of the claim that Roman Catholicism is the church that Jesus founded. Technically speaking, the Jerusalem church is the communion that Jesus founded. Jesus never ministered in Rome, and all His followers started out in the environs of Israel's center of political and liturgical life. If any church would seem to take pride in place, it would be the one where Jesus actually preached and ministered to His followers. But Roman Catholics do not concede the priority of Jerusalem to Rome. Nor do apologists mention that technically, Eastern Orthodoxy, which is the communion in which Jerusalem has historically resided, preceded Roman Catholicism. Technically speaking, Christianity originated not in Europe but in the ancient Near East. Christianity started as an Eastern and ancient religion, not as a Western and medieval one. To be sure, Roman Catholicism is older than Protestantism in Western Christianity. But in Christianity proper, Rome comes after Eastern Orthodoxy. For some reason, Roman Catholic apologists never take their historical claims to a logical end.

What Was the Church That Jesus Founded Like?

Jean-Guenolé-Marie Daniélou was a Jesuit French church historian who made his name in part by studying the ancient church. Pope John XXIII recognized Daniélou's gifts by making him one of the theological advisors to the Second Vatican Council. With Henri Marrou, another French Roman Catholic historian, Daniélou authored *The Christian Centuries,* a two-volume history of the Christian church. The opening chapters of this book put the claim that Rome was the church Jesus founded to the test.

First, Daniélou and Marrou use the book of Acts as the primary source for understanding the earliest days of the church. Jerusalem was the first church to which Luke applied the word *ecclesia* in the book of Acts. These Christians met together in private houses for worship—to break bread. These meetings were frequent and generally occurred on Saturday nights, the beginning of the eighth day, or the Lord's Day. The services featured instruction from the apostles, the breaking of bread (the Eucharist), and then prayer (2:42). The book of Acts also reveals an economic organization of the first Christians (4:32), with some question over the inclusion of Hellenist Christians within this structure and the subsequent appointment of deacons to care for the Hellenist widows (6:1–4). Daniélou and Marrou comment that the church relied on the work of elders (presbyters) and appointed James the Just with the preeminent position among that body. They even claim that James was "certainly head of the Jerusalem community."[2] James was both "president of the local college of presbyters and heir to the apostolic powers." This assertion is in tension with their additional remark, which includes no reference to Acts, that Peter appeared as head of the apostles. Even so, the authors make no reference to the papacy or to Christ's remark that He would build his church on Peter, the rock (Matt. 16:18). Apparently the church that Jesus founded in Jerusalem had James as its bishop, according to respected Roman Catholic historians.

After the formation of the Jerusalem church, Daniélou and Marrou turn to the spread of Christianity outside Palestine, mainly in Jewish circles. They cover Samaria, Antioch, Perga, Attalia, and Lystra. When Rome finally draws these historians' attention, it does so

---

2. Jean-Guenolé-Marie Daniélou and Henri Marrou, *The Christian Centuries,* vol. 1: *The First Six Hundred Years* (London: Darton, 1978), 13, 15, 16.

not in connection with Peter but with Paul, who in AD 44, according to Eusebius, traveled to Rome. In fact, Paul's evangelism among Gentiles was partly responsible for allowing Christianity to shed some of its initial Jewish identity and find a home outside Jerusalem—which was pivotal since Jerusalem fell as the center of Jewish life with the AD 70 destruction of the temple. Even so, Jerusalem was the home for the church's first council, the one recorded in Acts 15, an indication that councils preceded popes, if someone wants to talk about what came first. At this council, the initial structures of authority are evident. Daniélou and Marrou observe in passing that Peter had "a special rank." But for the workings of the church, the hierarchy consisted of two groups. First was the Twelve, the apostles who over time included Paul as one of their company. This was a body with which all Christians needed to be in communion. The other part of church government was the local hierarchy of Jerusalem, the council of elders, with James at their head.

Daniélou and Marrou also include in their account that significant encounter between Peter and Paul at Antioch, where the tensions between Jewish and Gentile Christians came into the open. In his letter to the Galatians, Paul recalled his rebuke of Peter "to his face" because "what he did was very wrong." According to Paul, in Antioch Peter ate with Gentile Christians and then stopped when James arrived because he "was afraid of criticism from these people who insisted on the necessity of circumcision." According to Daniélou and Marrou, the question was less about Peter's cowardice (though his denial of Christ would imply the apostle had possessed timidity under pressure) than about which way Christianity was heading. Paul believed the church needed to be freed from its Jewish origins. But Peter feared that Jewish nationalism in Jerusalem might lure Jewish Christians back to Judaism.[3] Either way, even if Peter's concerns were less personal than they were churchly, the conflict and the orientation of Paul's and Peter's ministries raises all sorts of questions about the historical claim that Peter was the first pope and that Roman

---

3. Daniélou and Marrou, *Christian Centuries*, 32.

Catholicism is the church that Jesus founded. Paul's ministry was to the Gentiles, and his epistle to the Romans indicates his concerns for that church. In contrast, Peter was much more oriented to the Jewish constituency of the early church. To conclude that Peter is a natural for bishop of Rome makes little sense. Indeed, when Daniélou and Marrou finally come to the origins of the Roman Church, they concede, "We have no information for the period following the persecution of Nero."[4] They add that the associations of the first church leaders in Rome are almost always with both Peter and Paul. Even into the second century, "little is known" about the church except that trophies to both apostles, Peter and Paul, are part of the historical record, with the memorial to Peter emerging as the one of preeminence.

The emergence of a system of episcopal government comes in the second century, as Daniélou and Marrou acknowledge, and in that system the bishop of Rome stands out as superior in rank. They write, "It is difficult to see in this…nothing more than the political and individual importance of the capital of the Empire."[5] But Thomas Bokenkotter, another Roman Catholic historian, though not disagreeing outright, leaves room for explaining Rome's authority as a function of the ancient world's social and political realities. Even aside from Rome's emergence as the chief bishop among the Western churches, Bokenkotter cannot help but notice that Paul's account of the early church's authorities leaves little room for a papacy. In the first epistle to Corinth, Paul writes of apostles, prophets, teachers, healers, and leaders. According to Bokenkotter, Paul's understanding of *apostle* included anyone whom Jesus had personally commissioned to preach the gospel. He also observes that Paul recognized "a certain primacy of the mother church," Jerusalem, but not to the point that diminished the apostle's own authority. Indeed, careful attention to the historical record that emerges from the New Testament shows that the emergence of bishops did not happen until the second century. Before that, elders and deacons directed the early church's governing

---

4. Daniélou and Marrou, *Christian Centuries*, 51.
5. Daniélou and Marrou, *Christian Centuries*, 110.

structures. Over time the churches needed one person to conduct worship and administer the sacraments, a process that led to the creation of monarchical bishops, who became "the focal point of the congregation."[6] These bishops became the norm by roughly 150 and took on responsibilities for correspondence, representing a congregation at regional assemblies, and having authority in decision-making. They attended some of the earliest councils that gathered in the Asian churches in the latter half of the second century.

Only later did some of the regional churches emerge as more authoritative than others at these assemblies. These "metropolitan churches" acquired status chiefly because of political circumstances. For example, the bishop at Rome "was granted a certain superiority" over other bishops in the region owing to his capacity to call synods and preside over discussions.[7] At the first ecumenical council, Nicaea, which met in 325, the bishops recognized three metropolitan churches—Rome, Alexandria, and Antioch. Rome's claim to superiority owed to the work that Peter and Paul carried out to found the church, its position as capital of the empire, and its wealth. Bokenkotter's point, to be sure, is not to settle the doctrinal claim that Rome is the church that Jesus founded. But his understanding of the historical record indicates that simple claims about Roman Catholicism being the original form of Christianity make no sense. Rome's standing among the other churches depended on a host of historical circumstances, both ecclesiastical and political. To recognize those developments is to understand that Rome became the center of the Western church while the Eastern churches had their own bishops with great authority. It is also to see that the pattern of episcopal rule, with Rome at the top in the West, was a much later development than Peter's first act after Christ's ascension. (For the historical origins of papal supremacy, see chapter 4.)

---

6. Thomas Bokenkotter, *A Concise History of the Catholic Church*, rev. ed. (2004; New York: Doubleday, 2005), 33.

7. Bokenkotter, *Concise History of the Catholic Church*, 35.

Non–Roman Catholic historians of the early church are no less skeptical of a view of church history that traces Rome's authority and status back to Jesus and Peter. Stuart George Hall, professor of ecclesiastical history at King's College (London), for instance, observes a feature of early assertions of papal primacy that Roman Catholic apologists often use against Protestantism—namely, that diversity and division are the consequences of not having a pope. According to Hall, one of the earliest Latin church fathers to argue for the importance of the papacy was Cyprian, the contested bishop of Carthage, who lived during the first two-thirds of the third century in north Africa. In the midst of persecutions by the Roman Empire around 250, Cyprian wrote one of his most significant works, *On the Unity of the Catholic Church*. At the heart of this treatise was an assertion of the church's universality (catholicity), which implied that the church was one in its scope. Cyprian was writing against the divisions that kept harming the church, whether the dissidents were in Rome or in Carthage. What ensured the church's unity was the mutual recognition of the bishops, who were responsible for maintaining and defending the rule passed down from the apostles. In other words, the episcopate, or the hierarchy, gave unity and authority to the church. Cyprian added to this brief on behalf of episcopacy a reference to the bishop of Rome, which later canon lawyers and theologians would use to prove the primacy of the pope, who was also the guarantor of church unity. What those church officials and contemporary apologists fail to include is that Cyprian retracted his claim about the primacy of Rome's bishop.[8]

Important to notice about Cyprian is that this argument for the pope, more implicit than explicit, comes almost two centuries after the ascension and the Council of Jerusalem. (Hall adds that the first real instance of papal power did not come until the fifth century with Leo I, who confronted the fall of the western half of the Roman Empire and used the papacy in part to pick up the pieces of social disorder that

---

8. Stuart George Hall, *The Doctrine and Practice in the Early Church* (Grand Rapids: Eerdmans, 1992), 90–91.

resulted from Rome's fall.)The early church may have regarded the Christians in Rome as significant because of their situation in the capital of the empire, though given the emperors' persecution of the church, the idea that believers had warm thoughts about the city of Rome is far-fetched (consider the way that non–New Yorkers think about New York City). But Rome was not the center of Christianity and only became that for Western Christians much later than the first century. Also significant is Cyprian's writing against disunity in the early church. Perhaps the papacy ensures church unity, though the practice of contemporary Roman Catholics defies that notion (see chapter 10). Perhaps the papacy gave institutional coherence to the ancient church in the western half of the empire. But contrary to the assertion that Rome is the church that Christ founded, which also implied order and unity from day 1 of church history, the early church was not united. Its organizational unity did not emerge until the fifth century and even then was more a claim by popes than the reality of church life. And the view of papal power that saw the papacy as the Vicar of Christ who ensured order throughout Christendom would have to wait for the twelfth and thirteenth centuries. To read the papacy of Leo I or Innocent III (who claimed supremacy over Europe's kings) back into Jesus's relationship with Peter is apologetical excess.

J. N. D. Kelly's *Early Christian Doctrines* has been a standard text for seminary students studying the ancient church. An Anglican who taught at Oxford, Kelly's assessments of the early church combined religious conviction and academic rigor. His assessment of the papacy's authority in the ancient church is mixed. On the one hand, among the patriarchates—Rome, Alexandria, Antioch, Constantinople, and Jerusalem—Rome held primacy of honor. Kelly asserts, "Rome's preeminence remained undisputed in the patristic period."[9] On the other hand, honor is different from authority. Kelly argues that the Eastern churches—the ones to which Jesus had direct ties—"never treated Rome as the constitutional centre and head of the church, much

---

9. J. N. D. Kelly, *Early Christian Doctrines* (New York: Harper, 1958), 406.

less as an infallible oracle of faith and morals." The Eastern churches also had little compunction in resisting Rome's direction. Here Kelly examines the way Eastern church theologians interpreted Matthew 16:18, the proof text that turns Roman Catholics into advocates of *sola Scriptura*, as if a biblical passage was sufficient to support church teaching. That passage, where Christ identifies Peter as a rock upon which the church will be built, indicated Peter's leadership and chief rank among the apostles. Chrysostom even called Peter "the mouthpiece of the apostolic company, the head of that band, the leader of the whole world, the foundation of the Church."[10] Even so, those same church fathers rarely attributed to Peter a rank superior to the other apostles. Cyril of Alexandria even interpreted the rock of Matthew 16 as Christ, while Chrysostom believed Christ merely indicated He would build the church on a faith like Peter's. The evidence suggests that the early church, at least in the East, regarded Peter as first among equals.

The Riddle of Canonical Authority

The early church's interpretation of New Testament passages later used to support papal supremacy raises a curious dilemma that surrounds questions about the relationship between biblical and church authority. Contrary to Roman Catholic apologists' claims that the church came before the Bible or that the bishops created the canon of Scripture, the historical record indicates that church leaders recognized the authority of the New Testament well before the papacy arose as the central locus of episcopal authority in the Western church. Estimates indicate that most church fathers recognized much of the New Testament by the late second century, even if it took until the fourth century for church councils to specify the contents of the biblical canon. Meanwhile, the authority of the papacy did not become apparent until the Roman Empire in the West fell in the fifth century, and the notions of papal supremacy and infallibility would have to wait for the twelfth and thirteenth centuries. If the question, as many

---

10. Kelly, *Early Christian Doctrines*, 407–8.

Roman Catholic apologists put it, is which came first, the easy answer is that the writings of the apostles came before the bishops and the authority that churchmen exercised.

Even so, the bigger question is why bishops and councils would recognize biblical authority if Scripture could become a source for undermining episcopal rule. If bishops believed they guaranteed the unity and truth of the church, why would they create a book they believed came from God that recorded the teachings and acts of the apostles Christ appointed, which subsequent readers could use to determine whether the bishops were following what God revealed? If they wanted to maintain their authority, even for edifying reasons, a book that rivaled their rule was a recipe for provoking challenges to the hierarchy—which is exactly what Luther did, but it was also the way Paul confronted Peter in Antioch.

This dilemma becomes even thornier when you consider how little the New Testament says about pieces of Roman Catholic teaching and practice that are nonnegotiable. If any figure dominates the New Testament other than Jesus Christ, it is the apostle Paul. Not only does he write more books than any other apostle but he winds up becoming the theologian chiefly responsible for explaining the relationship between Christianity and the Old Testament. According to J. Gresham Machen, Jesus himself had not given careful instruction on how Gentiles should be included in the company of His disciples. The relationship between Judaism and Christianity was indeed a delicate and difficult one, a challenge that hampered even the apostle Peter, who was uncertain about the requirements of the Torah when it came to being a disciple of Christ. But Paul provided the theological breakthrough. According to Machen, "The true state of the case may therefore be that Jesus by His redeeming work really made possible the Gentile mission, but that the discovery of the true significance of that work was left to Paul." Machen adds, "Gentile freedom, and the abolition of special Jewish privileges, had not been clearly established by the words of the Master."[11] For that reason, the church still needed "the epoch-making work of Paul" as the first theologian of the church.

The apostle Paul's achievement certainly challenges the view that Peter, as the first pope, was the one to give doctrinal stability and organizational unity to the first generation of Christians. In fact, Luke's narrative in Acts once again points in the direction of Paul's importance. To be sure, the first half of Acts centers on the church in Jerusalem and gives prominence to the original apostles, including Peter. But the second half of the book follows the missionary journeys of Paul. Luke concludes his narrative with Paul, not Peter, in Rome. The man who first persecuted Christians now finds himself in prison at the mercy of the Roman Empire. But aside from that biographical irony, the story of the early church told in the New Testament moves from the Gospels and the narratives of Christ's ministry, teaching, death, and resurrection to Acts, with the ascension, the church in Jerusalem, and the mission of Paul. If Rome and Peter were so much at the heart of the early church and so necessary to the future of Christianity, why is the New Testament so remarkably silent about Peter after Acts 15? Why does Paul not even mention Peter in his epistle to the Romans? And why did the apostle Peter write so little compared to Paul's intricate epistles? The New Testament certainly treats not Peter, who is supposed to be the model for his episcopal descendants in Rome, but Paul as the theological authority of the first generation of Christians.

Not to be missed is that the task of establishing the basic structures of church government fell not to Peter but to Paul. Apologists for the papacy and how crucial it is to church unity and wholesome doctrine rarely notice that when Paul gives instructions to Timothy in the Pastoral Epistles, he says nothing about Peter, the bishop of Rome, or the magisterium. In *Catholicism and Fundamentalism* Karl Keating goes out of his way to appeal to Matthew 16:18 to explain Peter's and the papacy's role in the early church, but he says nothing

---

11. J. Gresham Machen, *The Origin of Paul's Religion* (New York: Macmillan, 1921), 13, 15.

about Paul or Timothy.[12] He fails to look at church planting in real time in the first decades after Christ's ascension. And what stands out in Paul's instruction to Timothy, if you begin with the idea that Peter is the rock upon which God will build His church, is the complete silence about Peter and Rome:

> A bishop then must be blameless, the husband of one wife, temperate, sober-minded, of good behavior, hospitable, able to teach; not given to wine, not violent, not greedy for money, but gentle, not quarrelsome, not covetous; one who rules his own house well, having his children in submission with all reverence (for if a man does not know how to rule his own house, how will he take care of the church of God?); not a novice, lest being puffed up with pride he fall into the same condemnation as the devil. Moreover he must have a good testimony among those who are outside, lest he fall into reproach and the snare of the devil. (1 Tim. 3:2–7)

If the bishop of Rome were so important to maintaining the witness and unity of the church, one would think Paul would tell Timothy to check in regularly with his superiors. He might also tell Timothy to make sure the other church officers in Ephesus respect the authority of the church in Rome. But Paul does nothing of the kind. In fact, he sounds much more Protestant than Roman Catholic when he also tells Timothy:

> All Scripture is given by inspiration of God, and *is* profitable for doctrine, for reproof, for correction, for instruction in righteousness, that the man of God may be complete, thoroughly equipped for every good work.

> I charge you therefore before God and the Lord Jesus Christ, who will judge the living and the dead at His appearing and His kingdom: Preach the word! Be ready in season and out of season. Convince, rebuke, exhort, with all longsuffering and teaching. For the time will come when they will not endure

---

12. Karl Keating, *Catholicism and Fundamentalism: The Attack on "Romanism" by "Bible Christians"* (San Francisco: Ignatius Press, 1988), 209–11.

sound doctrine, but according to their own desires, because they have itching ears, they will heap up for themselves teachers; and they will turn their ears away from the truth, and be turned aside to fables. (2 Tim. 3:16–4:4)

Scripture is clearly central to pastoral ministry and church oversight, as Paul conceived it. He does not pull rank and talk about his status as an apostle, which he is even reluctant to do in 2 Corinthians, or tell Timothy to submit to his authority as one of the chosen.

This makes you wonder that if Peter were as important to the early church as Roman Catholics argue, why did Paul not understand that, and why did he fail to communicate even a partial understanding of Rome's priority in church affairs? One plausible answer is that Peter and Rome were simply not as central to another apostle who was inspired by the Holy Spirit and set up churches across the Mediterranean world.

The same point could be made about the immaculate conception and bodily assumption of Mary, one of only two infallible dogmas declared under the aegis of papal authority. If these doctrines about Mary are so much a part of the gospel and are crucial to Christian devotion, why did Paul, Peter, and John fail to mention Mary in their epistles to the early church? Outside the historical narratives of the New Testament, the biblical authors never mention Christ's mother, a striking omission considering how central Marian piety is to Roman Catholics. How could it be that the early church, in arguably the most representative historical documents we have (also inspired and inerrant), received no instruction from the apostles about the veneration of Mary or the aspects of her life that set her apart from all other followers of Christ? This is another one of those instances when silence is deafening.

The contrast between Rome and the New Testament becomes even more glaring in the context of the oft-repeated claim that the church came before the Scripture, not the other way around. What usually follows is the claim that Protestants merely look to Scripture while Roman Catholics follow the example of the early church. After stating that Rome regards no authority to be higher than Scripture,

Bryan Cross, a convert to Roman Catholicism, apologist, and theologian, goes on to bring Protestantism up short for failing to be in line with the early church:

> If, however, we allow the early Church to inform us regarding what are the Church's principles concerning soteriology, we find, for example, an overwhelming consensus among the Church Fathers that we are regenerated through baptism. We find a complete agreement between the Council of Trent and the Second Council of Orange.... And when we look at all the purported proof-texts for the Protestant notion of "faith alone," we find that they do not necessitate being interpreted in the Protestant way, and, when interpreted within the Apostolic Tradition handed down by the Church Fathers, we find that they are not only compatible with but even made more intelligible within this Tradition.[13]

What Cross fails to consider is that Scripture is both early church and word of God. How can you find anything more representative of the early church than the New Testament itself? Its contents not only reflect the outlook of the most important first Christians—namely, the apostles from whom the bishops claim to receive their authority—but the early church viewed these texts as the word of God.

To claim the mantle of the church that Christ founded, Roman Catholics either have to ignore history or ignore the problem that the writings of the apostles pose to the appeal to originalism. If Roman Catholicism is the original Christianity, why does the Bible contain so little of what Roman Catholics believe to be so important—papal infallibility and the perpetual virginity of Mary. And if apostolic succession is so important for the authority of bishops, why do not those same bishops have a higher regard to make sure their teachings conform to the authoritative writings of the apostles? To be sure,

---

13. Bryan Cross, "Authentic and Inauthentic Reform: A Brief Response to Reformanda Initiative's 'Is the Reformation Over: A Statement of Evangelical Convictions,'" *Called to Communion* (blog), November 3, 2016, http://www.calledtocommunion .com/2016/11/authentic-and-inauthentic-reform-a-brief-response-to-reformanda -initiatives-is-the-reformation-over-a-statement-of-evangelical-convictions/.

Christianity developed over time. Some of those developments could be wholesome and some damaging, though admitting error on the part of the church has always been a challenge for Roman Catholics. That is why the Reformed creeds added, as the Westminster Confession of Faith states, "All synods or councils, since the Apostles' times, whether general or particular, may err; and many have erred. Therefore they are not to be made the rule of faith, or practice; but to be used as a help in both" (31.4). But to hear Roman Catholic apologists explain it, the early church simply received the instruction of Christ and went merrily into the future without the slightest bit of a problem. That is, it went along pleasantly until those dissenters, those Protestants, upset the peace and harmony of the medieval church's reception of the early church.

Those who want to look at history that way may have a future writing screenplays for Hollywood that end happily ever after. Rather than settling debates, the Roman Catholic appeal to history only leads to more questions. With fifteen hundred more years of history than Protestantism, Roman Catholics have a whole lot more explaining to do. History is not reassuring or comfortable. If anything, history makes claims to certainty and authority look profoundly contested.

IS PROTESTANTISM DIVIDED?

Lay Roman Catholic speaker and apologist Hector Molina explains what Roman Catholics mean when they profess that the church is one:

> The Catholic Church is one in its faith (doctrine): the Church professes the one faith that has been passed down from the Apostles (what we Catholics refer to as the deposit of faith).
>
> The Church is one in its worship (sacraments): the Church celebrates in common the seven sacraments that were instituted by Christ, especially the Eucharist.
>
> The Church is one in its leadership (the pope): through the sacrament of Holy Orders, the Church's apostolic succession ensures uninterrupted continuity with the teaching and leadership of St. Peter (the pope) and the Apostles (the bishops) in union with him.[1]

But is the church one in the language it uses? It is a problem that almost every church faces. If a Presbyterian denomination in the United States wants to cooperate and even unite with a Reformed communion in Mexico, the problems it faces are not simply border crossings—long lines at the immigration kiosk in Rio Grande City or the customs checkout at Mexico City's International Airport. Even if church officers can assemble conveniently, they will likely have problems unless they are bilingual. In other words, how do

---

1. Hector Molina, "On Your Marks: The Church Is One," Catholic.com, June 21, 2013, https://www.catholic.com/magazine/online-edition/on-your-marks-the-church -is-one.

American church officers provide oversight to a communion that uses a different language and in which most of its members do not speak English? Conversely, how do Mexican Presbyterians know whether the instructions from American denominations are sound if they cannot understand the language in which such teaching comes? Church unity is a nice ideal. For Christians, it registers in human sentiments alongside ending hunger, poverty, and war. But the problems of unity go deeper than the kind of animosity or selfishness that informs the world's great afflictions. You may be able to blame war on national pride or a lack of charity. But can you attribute a failure to understand Spanish to sinful motivations? Since God Himself introduced the diversity of human tongues at the Tower of Babel because He saw the dangers of sinful humans uniting to consolidate power, to insist that unity (institutional or organizational) is a necessary characteristic of Christianity is to ignore something basic to human existence—namely, the diversity of tongues that God instituted.

Once upon a time, Roman Catholicism could escape the challenge of linguistic diversity by conducting its affairs in Latin. That language was not the one spoken by bishops and pastors in the East, where Greek provided the means of communication. As Roman Catholic polemicist Brian Kelly explains: "We should know that the Apostles all spoke Greek in addition to their native Aramaic. It was the language of education and business. In Galilee (Galilee of the Gentiles as it was known in Palestine) a Jew had to know Greek if he wanted to talk to a gentile. Perhaps our Lord Himself spoke Greek with the Roman centurion and Pilate. In the synagogues the Jews read from the Hebrew translation of the Greek translation (the Septuagint) of the Old Testament."[2]

That point about the language of Jesus and the apostles puts the question of the church that Jesus founded in a different light. It would certainly seem to give precedence to the Eastern Orthodox since they

---

2. Brian Kelly, "Why Does (Did) the Roman Catholic Church Make Latin Her Language?," *Catholicism.org*, September 18, 2014, http://catholicism.org/why-does-did -the-roman-catholic-church-make-latin-her-language.html.

use the language that Jesus likely spoke and in which the New Testament writings came, except perhaps for the gospel of Matthew, which may have been written originally in Aramaic. Kelly also observes that when Peter arrived in Rome, the Jewish Christians there "spoke Greek" and "offered Mass in Greek."[3] Only later did Latin emerge as the official language of the church, just as only later did the bishop of Rome come to dominate the Western church. Indeed, not until Jerome's translation of the Greek New Testament into Latin (382), which became the Vulgate (the standard biblical text for Roman Catholics—as it were, their King James Version), did Latin begin to emerge as the standard language of Western Christianity. But Greek was still very much the theological standard for Christianity if you consider that the great ecumenical councils debated and arrived at orthodox teachings on the Trinity and Christology by using Greek. That explains why many Greek words achieved importance even after Latin became the standard for the West. Only in the sixth century did Latin become the norm for Rome's liturgy. Many Greek words found their way into church Latin on account of their theological and scriptural importance.

So important has Latin been to Roman Catholicism—the way that Arabic is crucial to Islam and the Qur'an—that Pope John XXIII could declare as late as 1962 that Latin was the church's "primary language," one that gave Christianity a nobility and dignity that was only "fitting" for a society formed by Christ, even though Latin was not the language of Jesus. John instructed the church on the eve of Vatican II that church business be conducted in Latin, "for this is a maternal voice acceptable to countless nations." He also insisted that the study of theology use Latin, the language "best calculated to safeguard the integrity of the Catholic faith." If faculty at Roman Catholic schools and colleges could not speak or write in Latin, "they shall gradually be replaced by professors who are suited to this task," and bishops should insist on this with "patience."[4]

---

3. Kelly, "Why Does (Did) the Roman Catholic Church."
4. "*Veterum Sapientia:* On the Promotion of the Study of Latin," Papal Encycli-

Not to be missed in the development of Latin as the official language of Roman Catholicism (Scripture, theology, liturgy, and church law) is that this divided the church between its Latin- and Greek-speaking sectors. John XXIII tried to skirt this unpleasant historical detail when in defense of Latin he asserted, "Since in God's special Providence this language united so many nations together under the authority of the Roman Empire—and that for so many centuries—it also became the rightful language of the Apostolic See." Indeed, Latin became the basis for "a bond of unity for the Christian peoples of Europe." But that also meant that Latin divided the West from the East. With language, division is natural. This means that even in the glory days of the early church—the time that Roman Catholic apologists use against Protestantism—the institutions of church government were disunited. The differences between the Greek and Latin quarters of the church were not that dissimilar to Mexican and American Presbyterians in the twenty-first century lacking a common language. They did not know what the other part of the church was doing because they could not understand the language of the other Christians. Without the same language, not to mention a common worship or an orthodox standard for doctrine, church government is difficult. The claim that the church is one even if it has no common language is simply wishful thinking.

East versus West

The history of the ancient church proves how challenging historical study can be. At the same time and in the same debates in which the church came to a definition of Trinitarian and christological orthodoxy (the relations among the three persons of the Godhead and between the human and divine natures of Christ, respectively), Christianity was at the mercy of a political contest that sometimes pitted bishops against councils, emperors against bishops, and councils against emperors. The old adage has it that observing the making of

cals Online, last updated February 20, 2017, http://www.papalencyclicals.net/John23/j23veterum.htm.

sausage might well put eaters off the food. The same wisdom applies to the making of orthodoxy. History shows that historical actors were hardly singular in their devotion while pursuing the truths of Christianity. The great contribution of the early church to the history of Christianity was the difficult work of trying to formulate mysteries surrounding the doctrines of God and Christ. The truths that Protestants take for granted in a simple catechetical answer, such as, "There are three persons in the Godhead, the Father, the Son, and the Holy Spirit, and these are one God, the same in substance, equal in glory," were hard-fought ideas that absorbed the early church for the better part of two centuries. (Imagine having debates over justification by faith alone that occupy three or four different generations of church assemblies.)

At the same time, the circumstances that allowed the church to affirm these truths as orthodox involved questions about authority within the church (councils in relation to bishops) and between church and state (bishops and councils in relation to the emperor). Complicating the picture further was the decline of the Roman Empire in the West and the rise of Constantinople as the center of political power within the remaining jurisdiction of the territory once consolidated by Rome. Debates over precious and vital truths about God were also the context for an emerging antagonism between the Greek- and Latin-speaking parts of the ancient church. No matter how much the apologists insist, the early church was hardly united. Unity was an ideal that could not overcome the distinct realities of the East and the West.

The early ecumenical councils could not simply decide on the truth about the nature of God without also attending to the governing structures of the church. Authority within the church was implicated in the Trinitarian debates about the relationship between God the Father and God the Son. The Arians, who believed that Christ was subordinate to God the Father, also affirmed that the church's rulers should be subordinate to the emperor. As Mark A. Noll explains, "The kingdom of the Son (the church) must be subordinate to the kingdom of the Father (the empire)." The Arians even raised the stakes by likening the emperor to the chief bishop, with "the bishops (as servants of the Son) [receiving] their authority derivatively from the emperor (as the servant of God)." For the orthodox party, equality within the Trinity also implied a parity of authority between church and empire. "Since the Son was consubstantial with the Father, so too the kingdom of the Son (the church) was of equal dignity to the kingdom of the Father (the empire)."[5] These two powers governed separate or independent realms, one ecclesial (the bishops) and the other civil (the emperor). A significant consequence of the Nicene Creed was its preservation of a degree of autonomy for the church from imperial control, a reality that became more pronounced in Western Christianity because of the geographical isolation of Rome's bishop from the emperor in Constantinople and to the weakening and eventual fall of the Roman Empire's western sector.

The Council of Nicaea also recognized those bishops and cities of greatest importance for organizing and consolidating the witness of the early church. Canon 6 of Nicaea instructed the churches that "the ancient customs in Egypt, Libya and Pentapolis prevail" and "that the Bishop of Alexandria have jurisdiction" in that part of the church, just as it was "customary for the Bishop of Rome" in its region. Nicaea also recognized the authority of Antioch's bishop in that part of Christendom. As such, the Council of Nicaea recognized Rome, Antioch, and Alexandria as the chief centers (patriarchates) in the early church. Non–Roman Catholics have interpreted this to mean that Rome shared authority with bishops in the East and that Rome was the bishopric that oversaw the church in the western territories. Roman Catholic apologists use canon 6 to show that Rome was the model for the other bishops and so prove the papacy's supremacy even in the early church. Canon 4 of Nicaea, though, might suggest a different picture of Rome's relationship to the rest of the church. It states that "a bishop should be appointed by all the bishops in the province," and, if this is not possible, at least three bishops should meet to agree on the

---

5. Mark A. Noll, *Turning Points: Decisive Moments in the History of Christianity* (Grand Rapids: Baker, 1997), 60.

new bishop and that those absent should send their wishes "in writing" before ordination.

If, as Roman Catholics have it, the bishop of Rome's approval determines the legitimacy of ordination, Nicaea's silence about the papacy in ordination is a mystery. The supremacy of Rome became even more contested at the Council of Constantinople in 381 when the bishops affirmed in canon 3 that the bishop of Constantinople "shall have the prerogative of honour after the Bishop of Rome because Constantinople is New Rome." That decree would seem to indicate that Rome took precedence among the metropolitan bishops. Bishops in the East interpreted the canon to mean merely that the papacy was "first among equals." The fifth-century pope Leo (I) the Great disputed the canon because it seemed to elevate Constantinople, the new imperial capital, above the older dioceses of Antioch, Alexandria, and Jerusalem. As debated as these canons of the first ecumenical councils may have been, their intentions and reception are a clear indication that the papacy was not the guarantee of unity for the early church. In fact, questions of episcopal authority could be divisive.

That was certainly evident at the next major ecumenical gathering, the Council of Chalcedon (451). Not only did orthodox bishops seek to undo what the Second Council of Ephesus had done by affirming the two natures of Christ (as opposed to one nature at Ephesus), they also further defined the jurisdictions of the major urban centers. Part of this clarification of church government involved granting Jerusalem a separate jurisdiction from Antioch. It also included elevating Constantinople to the rank of a metropolitan bishop. In canon 28 the bishops declared: "The bishop of New Rome shall enjoy the same honour as the bishop of Old Rome, on account of the removal of the Empire. For this reason the [metropolitans] of Pontus, of Asia, and of Thrace, as well as the Barbarian bishops shall be ordained by the bishop of Constantinople." This canon has generated much debate by both Roman Catholic and Orthodox theologians and bishops, but one important piece of this decree is the recognition that a bishop's status depended on his proximity to the seat of power. Rome may

have enjoyed a special rank among bishops because it was the imperial capital. But with the center of power in the empire shifting to
Constantinople, Rome now had to share that unique status with the
bishop of Constantinople. Questions of which bishop Jesus appointed
were not uppermost in the stated reasons for deciding this question.

At the same time, the Council of Chalcedon also elevated
the bishop of Rome's importance since the bishops in the east—
Alexandria, Antioch, and Constantinople—looked to Rome to help
broker the disputes within their churches. The theological disputes
over the human and divine natures of Christ pitted Alexandria against
Antioch throughout much of the early church. Because the bishop
of Constantinople had access to the emperor and the civil authority
was the one most often calling for the ecumenical councils and the
one enforcing them, Constantinople had some say in resolving these
disputes. But its relatively new standing prevented Constantinople's
position from being decisive. For that reason, the Eastern bishops
appealed to Pope Leo I to settle the controversy about Christ. The language of Leo's *Tome* relied on previous agreements that implemented the
correct Latin words to communicate the meaning of key Greek terms
(e.g., *substantia* for *ousia*). But even though Leo's theological formula-
tions tipped the balance at Chalcedon, the Eastern bishops were slow
to recognize or approve of his words. Noll observes that the pope
was not pleased with Constantinople's challenge as the "New Rome."
He adds that "throughout the East at this time, respect rather than
deference marked the general attitude toward the bishop of Rome."[6]
Indeed, canon 28 further antagonized Leo.

That rivalry at Chalcedon between Rome and Constantinople
set into motion the eventual split (or schism) of 1054 between the
Eastern and Western churches. W. H. C. Friend observes that "politics rather than religion postponed the final schism of 1054."[7] At the
same time, although the East and West remained united—though
administratively more decentralized or federated than uniform

---

6. Noll, *Turning Points*, 74.

7. W. H. C. Friend, quoted in Noll, *Turning Points*, 76.

and consolidated—until the eleventh century, the Latin and Greek churches had distinct emphases that contributed to the split of 1054.

For instance, the West was much more practical and specific compared to the East's speculative tendencies. The church historian Henry Bettenson notices this difference as early as 96 in the Epistle of Clement (from Rome to Corinth), in which the bishop of Rome evinced characteristics of the Latin church: "Here we find no ecstasies, no miraculous 'gifts of the Spirit,' no demonology, no preoccupation with an imminent 'Second Coming.'"[8] That tendency was also evident in the different ways that theologians in the East and West approached philosophy. For Tertullian, the author of the famous query "What hath Jerusalem to do with Athens?" philosophy was a form of folly unless it acknowledged the truth of Christ and the gospel. (Tertullian drew support for this contention from the apostle Paul who in 1 Corinthians contrasted the "wisdom" of the Greeks with the folly of the cross.) Tertullian's Eastern counterpart, Clement of Alexandria, argued that philosophy was a form of preparation for the gospel, just as the law had shown to the Jews the need for a savior. In other words, Tertullian was more interested in arriving at truths that could give clarity (*regula fidei*) while Clement was interested in exploring the mysteries of Christianity with whatever tools were available, including the rich philosophical tradition of the Greek world. In some ways, these regional churches simply played out those traits that characterized the civilizations in which they had emerged. The Romans were known for virtues that cultivated the active life—a life of hard work, discipline, and service to the republic. Greeks, in contrast, construed the good life as one of contemplation in which philosophy as part of a life of leisure equipped a person for virtue. To be fair, these contrasts are tendencies more than opposing characteristics since the great accomplishment of Nicene orthodoxy—that is, the doctrine of the Trinity—drew heavily on Greek words and philosophy and yet produced the kind of doctrinal rule that Tertullian advocated.

---

8. Henry Bettenson, quoted in Noll, *Turning Points*, 134.

Even so, the Eastern and Western churches not only spoke different languages but reflected distinct religious expectations that prevented a collective identity from emerging across the church in the Mediterranean world. According to the Orthodox bishop and historian Timothy Ware:

> The Latin approach was more practical, the Greek more speculative; Latin thought was influenced by juridical ideas, by the concepts of Roman law, while the Greeks understood theology in the context of worship and in the light of the Holy Liturgy. When thinking about the Trinity, Latins started with the unity of the Godhead, Greeks with the threeness of the persons; when reflecting on the Crucifixion, Latins thought primarily of Christ the Victim, Greeks of Christ the Victor; Latins talked more of redemption, Greeks of deification.

Ware adds that from the seventh century on, once the churches became more isolated, the two sides of the "universal" church "were becoming strangers to one another—with no political and little cultural unity, with no common language." This meant the East and West faced the real possibility of following their "own approach in isolation and [pushing] it to extremes."[9]

The rise and spread of Islam from the seventh century on was, indeed, a significant circumstance in further increasing the differences between the Christian East and West. On the one hand, the expansion of Islam in parts of the old Roman Empire that had gone into decline made communication difficult between the eastern and western sectors of the medieval church. On the other hand, the threat to the remaining parts of the Roman Empire in the East hurt assistance to Rome militarily and economically from Constantinople and forced the papacy to look north to Europe's emerging monarchs for assistance in thwarting hostile threats to its political sovereignty. As Noll observes, "The vigorous presence of Islam in the Mediterranean was a most important factor in sundering the church." He adds, "Even if the will had existed to bridge East-West, Greek-Latin, patriarchal-papal

---

9. Timothy Ware, quoted in Noll, *Turning Points*, 135.

differences within Christianity, the strain in politics, military affairs, trade, and communications that an expanding Islam exerted on both parts of the church would probably have been too great."[10] The seizure of territory by Muslims surrounding Jerusalem, Antioch, and Alexandria left Rome and Constantinople as the only metropolitan bishops remaining to vie for supremacy within the church. Some argue that Islam also played a role in the eighth- and ninth-centuries' controversy over icons. The Seventh Ecumenical Council of Nicaea (787), for instance, approved the use of icons over against imperial bans on their use, a political effort to accommodate Muslim convictions. Although Rome received and accepted the provisions of that council, it was the last ecumenical council to be approved by the Eastern patriarchates. (Roman Catholicism recognizes an additional fourteen ecumenical councils.)

Eastern Christians had reasons to suspect that believers in the West did not receive the provisions of the ecumenical councils, however, when as early as 589, the Third Council of Toledo ruled to alter the Nicene Creed to include the phrase "and the Son" when reciting the article "We believe in the Holy Spirit who proceeds from the Father." At least since the eleventh century, the West has used this phrase. Although the idea that the Spirit proceeded also from the Son was a teaching of church fathers in both the Latin and Greek sources, it became controversial from the seventh century on as the rivalry between East and West became pronounced. The council in Spain that adopted this phrasing reflected the interaction between Christians of the West with pagan tribes in Europe, specifically the conversion of the Visigoths and their eventual rejection of Arianism in favor of Nicaea. The Council of Toledo was a local gathering, but its Trinitarian assertions became more and more the norm among Western Christians in Europe, and that, in turn, prompted the papacy to incorporate *filioque* into the West's version of the Nicene Creed. Again, the political dynamics of the West—that is, the need of the bishop of Rome to secure friendly relations with European

---

10. Noll, *Turning Points*, 119.

kings—was a factor in the normalization of *filioque*, though theological and historical reasons existed for its approval.

By the eighth century, when the spread of Islam was already alienating the East and the West, Popes Hadrian I and Leo III, who were in office between 772 and 816, faced the dilemma of competing demands over *filioque*. On the one hand, the phrase became a part of the official liturgy in the churches of the Franks, including Charlemagne. On the other hand, Byzantine emperors, beginning with Constantine V (767), strongly opposed departures from the original version of the creed. In fact, Leo III, who crowned Charlemagne in 800 as the Holy Roman emperor, had to confront charges from the Eastern church that the French king was a heretic for using *filioque*. With divided allegiances, one to his political ally in the West and one to his ecclesiastical brothers in the East, Leo walked a fine line but refused to approve *filioque* while also resisting calls for condemnation. Such papal diplomacy is an indication that the bishops of Rome lacked the kind of supreme power that papal apologists regularly claim. It was also part of a period of liturgical history in which the churches in Rome did not even include the creed in worship because they were unwilling to take a side between the West's and the East's emperors. In 1014, when Pope Benedict VII finally approved the use of the creed with *filioque* in worship, the reason owed greatly to the papacy's dependency on European monarchs for protection and social order. When King Henry II of Germany was in Rome for his coronation as Holy Roman emperor and was surprised that the creed was not part of the liturgy, Benedict accommodated the king and approved the amended creed for use in the West's worship.

Rather than ensuring the unity of Christendom, the papacy was caught up in the local circumstances—political, theological, and cultural—that prevented uniformity from prevailing in the early and medieval church. In fact, the eventual decisive split between the East and West in 1054 was as much a function of papal claims to supremacy as it was the culmination of existing tensions.

1054 and All That

The specific events that led the Eastern (Constantinople) and Western (Rome) churches to sever ties were important in themselves but also made sense of tensions that had been building for centuries. On the one hand, the papacy—with assistance from the Holy Roman emperor, in this case the German ruler Henry III—began to assert its authority over church life. In the eleventh century this meant forbidding the practice of simony (acquiring church offices by money) and enforcing the ideal of celibacy for priests. On the other hand, the increasing vigor of the pope—in this case Leo IX—also ran up against the political rivalry between the Eastern and Western emperors. This competition came to a head when the Normans, a European clan, threatened territory in Italy that belonged to Henry III, Leo IX, and the Eastern emperor, Constantine IX. The negotiated alliance among the emperors and pope to defeat the Normans required the remaining Greek churches in Italy to come under the authority of the pope. The patriarch of Constantinople, Michael Cerularius, who had a low opinion of the papacy, retaliated by demanding that the Latin churches in Constantinople conform to the Greek liturgy. (In both of these cases, the *filioque* clause in the Nicene Creed would have been an issue and a sign of whether a church leaned toward the East or the West by virtue of its liturgy.) The Latin churches refused Cerularius's demand and added to the antagonism.

In 1053 the difficult situation took on a more dramatic nature when the Normans invaded Rome and captured Leo IX. He dispatched diplomats to Constantinople for assistance. During this trip, Leo died, but that did not stop Cardinal Humbert, one of the pope's negotiators, from telling the patriarch of Constantinople that the bishop of Rome had "an unfettered jurisdiction over the whole Church."[11] Cerularius rejected the assertion, and Humbert responded by storming into the Hagia Sophia and placing on the altar a bull that excommunicated the patriarch. That was the precise moment of the Great Schism between the East and the West. It only became more

---

11. Noll, *Turning Points*, 133.

pronounced in the thirteenth and fifteenth centuries when synods met to heal the division, only to be rejected by the Orthodox Church.

The division between East and West is not an excuse for disunity among Protestants. But for critics of the Reformation to suggest that Protestantism alone bears responsibility for upsetting the unity of Christ's church is to be a 1054 denier. If the oldest parts of Christianity could not remain united, then why hold Protestants to a different standard? And if the division of 1054 took place for reasons that often had more to do with politics and culture than with theology or devotion, perhaps Roman Catholic apologists can hold the Reformers' spiritual concerns in higher regard; in fact, the sort of imperial politics that lurked in the background of 1054 point once again to the corruption of the church because of its worldly ambitions and the Reformers' laudable effort to order the church according to the Word of God, not according to civilization or political order. When Christian Smith writes to evangelicals to prompt them to consider converting to Rome and "you notice in a new way how thoroughly and deeply the visible Christian church is divided" and "that starts to bother you," you may also have to wonder how Smith can be so glib about joining a church that is separated from the oldest centers of Christian ministry.[12] Could it be that unity is simply the club with which to beat Protestants? Division is certainly not a reason to remain outside Roman Catholicism. In a manner that would make positive thinkers proud, Smith blithely tells would-be Roman Catholics that the "division of Christendom is in the active process of being healed." His optimism even extends to a bumper sticker bromide, "Full reconciliation is possible within our lifetime." Such powers of positive thinking, however, do not apply to 1517. The Reformation makes "the Catholic church weak" and causes Rome to fail "to be and do what it could and should." For this reason, the Reformation should not be celebrated but instead calls for "sorrow, repentance, and reconciliation."[13] If not for selective apologetical purposes, the same should be said about 1054, and no one interested

12. Smith, *How to Go*, 28.
13. Smith, *How to Go*, 111.

in church unity should become a Roman Catholic until Rome rees-
tablishes full relations with the Eastern churches. That, at least, is as
much an implication of the apologist's argument as it is a critique
of Protestantism.

But the issue of who's to blame for division still does not address
the nature of church unity. Having one church requires having one
language, as noted in the introduction to this chapter. Without a single language that allows for all believers and church officers to be on
the same page literally, the ideal of church unity is always going to rely
on the sort of nods and winks that go with diplomacy at the United
Nations. In fact, until human beings overcome the divisions God
Himself instituted at the Tower of Babel, when the way to prevent
united humankind was to introduce a diversity of tongues, church
unity will be something for which to hope when the new heavens
and new earth appear. Not even the pouring out of the Holy Spirit
at Pentecost removed the barriers caused by a diversity of languages.
Those gathered, according to the account in Acts 2:6, "were confused,
because everyone heard them speak in his own language." As long as
believers inhabit different nations and speak different languages, the
better idea for understanding church unity is not to wish for one central government or one Christian capital city but to recognize, as the
idea of subsidiarity teaches, that local church government is better
than top-down authority. Subsidiarity is an idea that Roman Catholics apply to politics and society. In a nutshell, its basic point is the
organizing principle that matters ought to be handled by the lowest
or least centralized competent authority, the one in closest proximity to the task at hand. That is exactly what Protestants wanted to
accomplish, and did. The Reformers wanted to take control of church
life away from the pope and restore it to pastors, councils, and local
bishops, the church officers closest to congregational life and best
equipped for pastoral care. Because churches err and believers are
fallen, those reforms still need to be implemented and extended. But
the idea of going back to the unity that comes with a monarchical
and infallible archbishop who lives in Italy is not a recipe for advanc-
ing Christ's kingdom. One could even argue that such reliance on a

single, all-powerful church officer had a lot to do with creating conditions that made reform necessary. That church division followed is largely a function of bishops whose pride and defensiveness prevented listening to criticism and hearing proposals for reform.

The ideal of church unity is a two-edged sword.

8

WHEN ORDINARY IS EXTRAORDINARY

Do Protestants lose church members because their buildings are so ugly? For anyone who has grown up in an average Protestant structure dating from the 1950s and then visited Europe and seen the impressive cathedrals that adorn the Continent's cities, the idea of worshiping in a space like England's Winchester Cathedral or Rome's St. Peter's Basilica is heady and even inspiring (never mind filling out the paperwork for immigration or finding a job). One website describes St. Peter's Basilica in Rome as a space that covers 5.7 acres, has a capacity for sixty thousand people, and displays "the finest Renaissance monuments and decorations money could buy, employing the talents of such greats as Michelangelo and Bernini."[1] In 1846 when Charles Dickens visited Rome and saw St. Peter's, he wrote, "The first burst of the interior, in all its expansive majesty and glory; and, most of all, the looking up into the Dome; is a sensation never to be forgotten."[2] This kind of experience explains why Agnes Howard took notice of American college students who encountered the beauty of Roman Catholic church architecture: "Young people raised in low-church, informal American worship spaces—functional ones, with lots of room for Sunday School and coffee hour and mid-week basketball fellowship—can feel awe when they encounter those European cathedrals. My husband and I have seen this reaction

---

1. "St. Peter's Basilica, Vatican City," Sacred Destinations, http://www.sacred-destinations.com/italy/rome-st-peters-basilica.

2. Charles Dickens, *Pictures from Italy and American Notes*, in *The Complete Works of Charles Dickens* (New York: Cosimo Classics, 2009), 107.

when accompanying students in Europe, many of them on first trips there…. The height, the vastness, the color, the symbolic richness are impressive." Howard goes on to describe the kind of questions that immediately follow the wonder inspired by cathedrals:

How does this church recognize the presence of God?

How does it move believers together around sacramental food, the hearing of the Word?

How does it physically connect us with people here, and here before—our parents, their neighbors, ancestors, dwellers on the lands, missionaries, the early church?

How does it invite others in?

Is it beautiful? Should it be?[3]

The contrast between Protestant and Roman Catholic church architecture is another of the objections that apologists for Rome use against the Reformation. Protestants, some critics complain, are merely functional in the way they design or use a building, which coincides with the modern world's preference for practicality (the shopping mall) over dignity (the village market). The former fundamentalist-turned-Roman-Catholic priest Dwight Longenecker says that modern architecture and Protestantism agree that "form follows function." "Ask what a building is for," he explains, "and you will know how it should be built." A garage houses a car; an office building enables people to work. For Protestants, a church is a place for people to gather for worship. As such, "seating should be comfortable," the pulpit should have good sight lines, and there should be a decent sound system and good heating and air-conditioning. Longenecker complains that Protestant churches are simply auditoriums—"large, comfortable, efficient" spaces for everyone to meet.[4]

---

3. Agnes Howard, "Why Is That Church So Ugly?," *Anxious Bench* (blog), Patheos, May 26, 2014, http://www.patheos.com/blogs/anxiousbench/2014/05/why-is-that -church-so-ugly/.

4. Dwight Longenecker, "On Church Architecture: Preaching Hall or Temple?," Catholic Exchange, July 8, 2014, http://catholicexchange.com/preaching-hall-temple.

Longenecker thinks that Roman Catholic architecture also follows function, but the purposes of a church building are much weightier than simply a comfortable, well-lit space to hear a sermon. A church is the place where God's presence "resides." People meet God at church. As such, architecture should reflect God's presence. According to Longenecker, "A church should be so beautiful that it points our hearts and minds not only to the presence of God here, but to [the] Holy of Holies in Heaven." Beauty points not simply to ornamentation in statues and painting, frescoes, and stained glass but also to architectural design. He believes that such structural beauty requires classical proportions, with arches and columns to match. The overall effect of a church building should be "a sermon in stone." It should communicate certain truths that also connote that Roman Catholicism is "beautiful and permanent and strong." "We do not install stained glass and mosaics and wall paintings and carvings just to make it look pretty," he adds. "All of these things reflect the beauty of God and the eloquent beauty of our Catholic faith." This kind of church building will connect today's believers with "the great Tradition" that stretches back "two thousand years."[5] Never mind that Christian cathedrals did not come along until emperors converted to Christianity, and don't think too hard about the churches that Christ founded that met in homes to hear the preached word and partake of the Lord's Supper. The comprehensive effect of church architecture done well, according to Roman Catholic logic, is to embody the divine in forms seen and touched. That sense of divine presence is what grabs the attention of American Protestants who visit Europe or older Roman Catholic parishes in the United States and tempts them to think this is a better way to worship God and to present their faith to the world. In other words, Protestants have a beauty deficit, and that deficiency is responsible in part for people leaving Protestant communions for Rome.

In point of fact, Protestantism's beauty problem is simply one more illustration of the huge divergence between Protestants and

---

5. Longenecker, "On Church Architecture."

Roman Catholics, an example that actually testifies to the genius of the Protestant Reformation. To be sure, Roman Catholic cathedrals are beautiful and can prompt a sense of wonder and awe. But the question that Roman Catholic apologists rarely ask is whether humans, even regenerate ones, can truly capture or exhibit God or His attributes in buildings, paintings, or statues. Might such an effort to portray God be an instance of the idolatry or blasphemy that the second commandment forbids? And what about the virtues of simplicity and ordinariness? Might Protestants have their own version of beauty, one that cannot rival the stunning display of a European cathedral but that in its own way testifies to the amazing story of salvation that God has revealed in Scripture? The answer is, of course, yes. Explaining that answer requires some reminders both about the doctrine of God and the way He revealed Himself to His people.

Doctrine of God 101

When and where Roman Catholics began to think that buildings, images, or statues could capture or convey God's presence is a mystery, but that willingness to identify God with certain physical things is a fundamental difference between Roman Catholicism and Protestantism. Where the former sometimes exhibits a tendency to make created order into one big sacrament, as if all creation is a means of grace, Protestants have stressed the transcendence of God in a way that underscores an essential distance between God the Creator and His creation and the gap between divine and human natures. For instance, Roman Catholics will often enlarge their understanding of grace or God's special or miraculous works to include common or ordinary aspects of human existence or the natural world. For instance, one Roman Catholic writer posits that we live in a sacramental world. This means

> quite simply, viewing the world as sacrament. A redundant definition it might be, but often times the simplest explanations are the best. If we do truly believe that the Sacraments are moments in time where the invisible grace of God is made visible and tangible then seeing this same grace working constantly in and

through our daily lives would only beg that we see the sacramental nature of daily life. This is not to say that every blade of grass is truly the transubstantiated body of Christ, but it does substantiate St. Ignatius's charge to see God in all things.[6]

Such an outlook can also involve a dismissal of Protestants as liberal or secular because they fail to see God in all things or see creation as merely natural without any traces of the being and essence of the divine. For instance, Tracey Rowland, an accomplished Roman Catholic theologian, contrasts Protestantism with Roman Catholicism as a basic difference over the fluidity between God and creation, or between the supernatural and the natural. After a visit to Scotland she wrote, "It can't be all that difficult to compete with liberal Calvinism and garden-variety New Age paganism when one has the full treasury of a sacramental Catholicism—a faith for which there is 'no separation,' no iron curtain standing between the sacred and the profane, no unbridgeable gulf between heaven and the Highlands."[7]

If an immanentizing of creation—stressing God's presence in all things—is the tendency of Roman Catholicism, Protestants have emphasized God's transcendence. The creeds of the Protestant churches display this characteristic when they affirm, as the Westminster Confession of Faith does, "There is but one only, living, and true God, who is infinite in being and perfection, a most pure spirit, invisible, without body, parts, or passions; immutable, immense, eternal, incomprehensible, almighty, most wise, most holy, most free, most absolute" (2.1). Such an understanding of God as infinitely beyond is also responsible for a doctrine of creation that stresses the wide gap between Creator and creature. As the Creator, God has no beginning and brings all things into existence as a manifestation of His glory. The natural world and even the world of invisible beings

---

6. Patrick J. Sullivan, "Seeing God in All Things: Living in a Sacramental World," *Ad Infinitum Blog*, November 8, 2012, http://www.catholicapostolatecenter.org/blog/seeing-god-in-all-things-living-in-a-sacramental-world.

7. Tracey Rowland, "Once Deeply Catholic, Modern Scotland Needs a Theological Revival," *The Catholic World Report*, April 28, 2016, http://www.catholicworldreport.com/2016/04/28/once-deeply-catholic-modern-scotland-needs-a-theological-revival/.

are not extensions of God or emanations of His existence. Creation depends on God but is not divine. It is created and finite.

For that reason, Protestants "secularized" what Roman Catholics had sacralized. Protestants demystified Christendom. They "disenchanted" a world that Rome had constructed as filled with sacred or redemptive meaning. In effect, Protestants did to European Christianity what Judaism had done to the pagan world—denied the divine-like qualities of things that were merely part of the created world. The sociologist Steve Bruce has been especially instructive on the parallels between ancient Judaism and Protestantism:

> The religions of Egypt and Mesopotamia were profoundly cosmological. The human world was embedded in a cosmic order that embraced the entire universe, with no sharp distinction between the human and the non-human. Greek and Roman gods even mated with humans. Such continuity between people and the gods was broken by the religion of the Jews. As Berger puts it: "The Old Testament posits a God who stands outside the cosmos, which is his creation but which he confronts and does not permeate." He created it and he would end it, but, between start and finish, the world could be seen as having its own structure and logic. The God of Ancient Israel was a radically transcendent God.... There was a thoroughly demythologized universe between human kind and God.[8]

Protestantism had a similar effect on Roman Catholic Europe. The Reformers insisted that the church could not contain or house God in a cathedral or even in the Mass. Critics of Protestantism object that the desacralization of the world led Western society away from God. What they fail to see is that Protestants also preserved the dignity, majesty, and mystery of God. The infinity, eternity, and immutability of God make Him distinct and infinitely beyond anything in the created world. It also, by the way, makes His salvation certain, not something that could change or decay the way creation does.

---

8. Steve Bruce, *God Is Dead: Secularization in the West* (Malden, Mass.: Blackwell, 2002), 6.

The doctrine of God was also responsible for Protestant objections to Roman Catholic worship. The Reformers took seriously those accounts in the Old Testament that revealed how frightening and even impossible it was for humans to enter God's presence. Moses's encounter with God at the burning bush—the logo for most Presbyterian denominations in Scotland and Ireland—is one instance of the awkwardness inherent when humans enter the presence of God. When Moses heard God's voice in the strange sight of a bush on fire and approached, God responded, "Do not draw near this place. Take your sandals off your feet, for the place where you stand is holy ground" (Ex. 3:5). For John Calvin, the holiness of that place was no indication of its inherent sacredness, as if the plot in which that bush grew would be forever consecrated. Instead, it was simply a place where God had "deigned to give…the sign of his presence." In fact, Calvin understood that God's nature as inherently spiritual (i.e., immaterial) meant that we should never "draw down God from heaven, and affix him to places on earth" or try to attribute "sanctity perpetual" to that "which is only temporary." Calvin explained, "Since the nature of God is spiritual, it is not allowable to imagine respecting him anything earthly or gross; nor does his immensity permit of his being confined to place." This was no less true for Mount Sinai, where Moses received God's law. The mountain itself did not become a holy place permanently because of that astounding encounter between God and man or because of the law's momentous significance in the history of redemption. As Calvin remarked, "Mount Sinai did not, therefore, naturally possess any peculiar sanctity." Instead, the place was special for the transaction between God and Moses because God condescended "to give there the sign of his presence."[9]

Moses's experience of the divine later at the same place, recorded in Exodus 33, is again instructive for considering God's nature and His presence with His people in worship. In that account Moses

---

9. John Calvin, *Commentaries on the Four Last Books of Moses*, trans. Charles William Bingham (1847–1850; repr., Grand Rapids: Baker, 1981), 1:64 (commentary on Exodus 3:4).

specifically asked if he could "see" the glory of God. God refused and said, "You cannot see My face; for no man shall see Me, and live." Instead, God placed Moses in the cleft of a rock and passed by so that Moses could see God's back rather than His face (Ex. 33:20–23). Calvin explains that no human, not even the holiest, could bear to stand in God's presence since His "incomprehensible brightness would bring us to nothing." For that reason, God refuses to allow "a complete knowledge of Him," but only what our "humble capacity" can bear. To see God was analogous to looking at the sun. No human being could do that but would need to be enclosed in a "fissure or hole" in a rock with a "narrow and oblique window, which so far admits the sun's rays as that one, who is shut up in a deep and obscure place, may receive some advantage from the light, yet never see the sun itself nor enjoy its brightness."[10] Looking directly at the sun, like entering into God's presence, would blind and consume any person, no matter how holy.

The Roman Catholic notion that a building or worship space should reflect God's presence and beauty is completely at odds with what Scripture teaches about the transcendence of God and the vast chasm that separates the Creator from His creatures. That gap is even more poignant given the existence of human sinfulness. "Who could possibly stand in God's presence?" as Psalm 24 asks. The answer the psalmist gives in verse 4 is,

> He who has clean hands and a pure heart,
> Who has not lifted up his soul to an idol,
> Nor sworn deceitfully.

This means that believers only enter into God's presence clothed in the perfect righteousness of Christ, imputed to them and received by faith alone.

The danger of entering God's presence was even apparent in the pattern of Old Testament worship, which in some way is the model for Roman Catholic services, with their priests, altars, and sacrifice

---

10. Calvin, *Commentaries on the Four Last Books of Moses*, 3:381–82 (commentary on Exodus 33:20).

in the Mass. Despite all the detailed instructions for the articles of the tabernacle and the obvious beauty they displayed, with materials as diverse as "gold, silver, and bronze; blue, purple, and scarlet thread, fine linen, and goats' hair; ram skins dyed red, badger skins, and acacia wood; oil for the light, and spices for the anointing oil and for the sweet incense; onyx stones" (Ex. 25:3–7), God refused to let the people see such beauty. Indeed, He gave specific instructions in Numbers 4:6–11 that the awe-inspiring articles of the tabernacle should be covered:

> Then they shall put on it a covering of badger skins, and spread over that a cloth entirely of blue; and they shall insert its poles.
>
> On the table of showbread they shall spread a blue cloth, and put on it the dishes, the pans, the bowls, and the pitchers for pouring; and the showbread shall be on it. They shall spread over them a scarlet cloth, and cover the same with a covering of badger skins; and they shall insert its poles. And they shall take a blue cloth and cover the lampstand of the light, with its lamps, its wick-trimmers, its trays, and all its oil vessels, with which they service it. Then they shall put it with all its utensils in a covering of badger skins, and put it on a carrying beam.
>
> Over the golden altar they shall spread a blue cloth, and cover it with a covering of badger skins; and they shall insert its poles.

Why would God command such exquisite execution of the interior of the tabernacle only to require Levites to cover up such beauty? The reason, according to Calvin, is to increase reverence for and fear of holy things. God did not want the people to be comfortable in the presence of a holy God, "for God threatens them with death if they touch any forbidden thing" and admonishes the priests "lest by their carelessness they should destroy their brethren." Anything the Levites left uncovered would be the cause of the people's destruction.[11]

To be sure, the rules governing worship after the coming of Christ, the nature of New Testament worship, is not bound by the

---

11. Calvin, *Commentaries on the Four Last Books of Moses*, 2:258–59 (commentary on Numbers 4:4).

same stipulations to which the Israelites were obligated. Christians do not make sacrifices, do not worship in temples, do not require priests to lead services, and do not have commands for how priests and parts of the sanctuary should look. Churches do not even have sanctuaries; they merely provide a place for the saints to assemble for the ministry of word and sacrament. Spaces are not sacred. But even when God did give specific instructions for creating beautiful spaces that might exhibit His presence, He also prevented such a display from being widely available. Only the high priest entered the holy of holies and did so only once a year. Rather than providing a biblical justification for constructing and decorating beautiful spaces for Christian worship, the Old Testament actually provides numerous prohibitions that taught the people not to revel in the beauty but to be reverent and submissive. Again, the reason is the enormous gulf between God and humankind because of the Creator-creature distinction and the wages of sin.

The sense of sinners entering the presence of a holy and righteous God was partly responsible for the way that Reformed Protestants interpreted the second commandment's ban on making images of God. Not only did the Reformation take seriously Calvin's idea that the human mind is a "factory of idols" and so prone to worship God in ways that fallen humans devise—creating a god in our image to be worshiped in a way congenial to us—but they also looked carefully at the prohibitions in the second commandment against making images of God—even of the second person of the Trinity, who took human form. Calvin writes about how subtle this temptation is to conjure up God according to our own imagination:

> Therefore, to devise any image of God, is in itself impious; because by this corruption His Majesty is adulterated, and He is figured to be other than He is. There is no need of refuting the foolish fancy of some, that all sculptures and pictures are here condemned by Moses, for he had no other object than to rescue God's glory from all the imaginations which tend to corrupt it. And assuredly it is a most gross indecency to make God like a stock or a stone.

Even if someone insists that an image is merely an adornment but not something to be revered, Calvin warned that as soon as a representation of God creeps in, people invariably and "superstitiously adore the work of their own hands." Indeed, the point of the second commandment was to underscore the nature of God as entirely spiritual, a being completely beyond human experience or comfort. Calvin explained, "The...worship of God must be spiritual, in order that it may correspond with His nature." And whenever humans endeavored to represent God or His presence, "they estimate Him according to their own reason, and thus in a manner metamorphose Him."[12]

But what about the fine and beautiful arrangements of the tabernacle? Did not the gold and precious stones used to equip the place of worship and the fine linens used for the priest's vestments indicate that God wanted His people to have a sense of beauty in worship? Calvin rejected that argument. First, this "exquisite workmanship" and these "costly materials" were not in the tabernacle to "feed [the worshipers'] eyes" with "empty pictures." Instead, the Israelites were to look on with "spiritual eyes of faith" and so "consider the glory more excellent than the whole world, which was there represented." Second, Calvin reminds us that Moses also received instructions to cover these objects in the tabernacle. Nothing "magnificent appear[ed] in the tabernacle to delight men's eyes, but rather was all its richness and excellence covered up with goats' hair and paltry leather, in order that believers beneath that hidden beauty might reflect on something higher than the carnal sense."[13]

Jesus gave instructions on the true nature of New Testament worship in His encounter with the Samaritan woman at the well in John 4. This lady knew that the Jews worshiped at a special place, the temple in Jerusalem, "the place where one ought to worship" (v. 20). Jesus responded that the time was coming, which His death, resurrection, and ascension would make possible, when "neither

---

12. Calvin, *Commentaries on the Four Last Books of Moses*, 2:108, 107, respectively (commentary on Exodus 20:4).

13. Calvin, *Commentaries on the Four Last Books of Moses*, 2:172 (commentary on Exodus 26:1).

on this mountain, nor in Jerusalem, [will you] worship the Father"
(v. 21). He added, "The hour is coming, and now is, when the true
worshipers will worship the Father in spirit and truth; for the Father
is seeking such to worship Him" (v. 23). If Roman Catholics like
Dwight Longenecker studied Scripture more than the aesthetics of
church architecture, they might pause over assertions that buildings
or places capture God's presence in the age of the Holy Spirit. This
was certainly the case for the writer of the epistle to the Hebrews,
who understood what Jesus tried to explain to the woman at the well:

> For you have not come to the mountain that may be touched
> and that burned with fire, and to blackness and darkness and
> tempest, and the sound of a trumpet and the voice of words,
> so that those who heard it begged that the word should not be
> spoken to them anymore....
>
> But you have come to Mount Zion and to the city of the liv-
> ing God, the heavenly Jerusalem, to an innumerable company of
> angels, to the general assembly and church of the firstborn who
> are registered in heaven, to God the Judge of all, to the spirits
> of just men made perfect, to Jesus the Mediator of the new cov-
> enant, and to the blood of sprinkling that speaks better things
> than that of Abel. (Heb. 12:18–20, 22–24)

Instead of trying to represent God's presence in a building
designed to make worshipers think they have entered a holy space,
the New Testament stresses worship that relies on God's Word and
the work of the Holy Spirit. When Jesus spoke of worshiping in spirit
and truth, He was pointing forward to His later instruction in John's
gospel that the Holy Spirit would lead the church into all truth. In
the present age of salvation, what could be more truthful and more
revealing of God's will than the words of Scripture that the Holy Spirit
inspired? And what could be more faithful to the Word-and-Spirit
nature of New Testament worship than services that feature Scripture read and preached? For Protestants, church architecture does not
suggest God's presence, but the invocation—"Our help is in the name
of the Lord"—lifts the saints from an ordinary room or building into
the heavenlies with all the saints and angels gathered before God's

throne. In such a setting, images, statues, arches, and columns—as beautiful as they may be—are no match for the beauty of God's holiness, revealed in Scripture and seen through the eyes of faith with the illumination of the Holy Spirit. Indeed, the centrality of the word for Protestant worship—what some dismiss as logocentrism—is precisely one of the Reformation's great achievements and is captured well in the Heidelberg Catechism's warning about images in worship:

96. Q. What does God require in the second commandment?

A. That we in no wise represent God by images, nor worship him in any other way than he has commanded in his word.

97. Q. Are images then not at all to be made?

A. God neither can, nor may be represented by any means: but as to creatures; though they may be represented, yet God forbids to make, or have any resemblance of them, either in order to worship them or to serve God by them.

98. Q. But may not images be tolerated in the churches, as books to the laity?

A. No: for we must not pretend to be wiser than God, who will have his people taught, not by dumb images, but by the lively preaching of his word.

If Protestants do not have beautiful churches, they may have good reasons. To begin with, money used to pay architects and painters or to buy materials can sustain missionaries, church planters, and pastors. Such an investment in evangelism and pastoral care is arguably much more crucial to the lives of believers than gazing at beautiful stained glass windows or hearing magnificent pipe organs. Even more important is Scripture's teaching about God, how He makes Himself known and what He has revealed as acceptable worship. Protestants' aesthetics may not measure up to the most sophisticated tastes of some Roman Catholics, but don't ever forget the kitsch—the statuary of the holy family, the sentimental images of Mary—that Roman Catholic laity buy and use to decorate their homes. But Protestants value the Word and trust in the Spirit. Through the Word read and preached and by the work of the Holy Spirit, people encounter God in a much more profound way than by entering a beautiful cathedral. That was the experience of the church that Jesus founded when for at least three centuries Christians met in homes and other makeshift settings to gather around God's Word.

When Ordinary Is Beautiful

To say that the point of the reform of worship during the Reformation was to make church less grand and more ordinary is to capture more than a grain of truth since Protestant piety was characterized by serving God in the common affairs of life. The Reformers self-consciously eliminated the rituals and trappings of Roman Catholic worship that called more attention to the church and her priests than to the glory of God. They also sought to make worship accessible to the laity by using the vernacular language of the people rather than Latin and by engaging the congregation more in the elements of the service. To many people these reforms destroyed the beauty and majesty of Rome's worship. But the Reformers not only questioned the biblical justification for such visible expressions of glory; they also understood that in the Christian era of the history of redemption, God's people were called to a vernacular and simpler form of devotion (the Latin Bible, the Vulgate, was once vernacular in the sense that it translated Scripture into the ordinary tongue of the Romans).

The characteristic components of Reformed worship reflect this twin commitment to the Bible's sufficiency in regulating worship, sometimes known as the regulative principle, and the value of simplicity in glorifying God. On the level of congregational participation, the Reformation introduced liturgical reforms that captured the imperative for all God's assembly to participate in worship rather than watching priests perform the service. One indication of lay participation was congregational singing. Aside from the question of exclusive psalmody or hymnody, Protestants were unanimous in promoting the entire congregation's singing of praise and thanksgiving. Not having sung before, the laity at the time of the Reformation faced a stiff challenge to participate in songs of praise. This is why the Reformers commissioned music that could be sung by the entire congregation, not simply by those gifted to sing in a choir.

Another element of worship in which the laity participated was the Lord's Supper. Aside from the enormous reform of teaching and practice that took away the Mass and returned the sacrament to its status as a meal, the administration of the Lord's Supper engaged the laity in ways unheard of within the Roman Catholic Church. Not only had the laity prior to the Reformation participated in the sacrament only once a year, but when they did they received only the bread because they might spill the wine, thus desecrating what was thought to be the blood of Christ. By introducing the observance of the Supper more frequently (at least four times a year in most Reformed churches) and by giving bread and wine to the laity, Protestant worship became more accessible than Rome's practice for the ordinary people of God.

The ministry of the Word also reflected an affirmation of the common in Reformed worship. Preaching was, first, in a known language. Unlike the Roman Catholic liturgy, which was in Latin and completely inaccessible to anyone beyond the learned elite, Reformed worship aimed to bring all people into full participation, even when they sat and listened to the word proclaimed. At the same time, by making preaching more central in worship than the Lord's Supper, the Reformers were following the apostle Paul's instruction about the means that God uses to bring people to faith and sustain them on their pilgrimage. As Paul conceded to the Corinthians, preaching appeared to be a foolish way—perhaps even vulgar from the Greeks' perspective—to proclaim the truth and goodness of Christ. But its simplicity was precisely the point because by virtue of its ordinary character, preaching would not let people take credit for salvation but showed that the power of the gospel was God alone.

Chapter 7.6 on the covenant of grace in the Westminster Confession of Faith captures well the ordinary element of Christian worship that the Reformation recovered:

> Under the gospel, when Christ, the substance, was exhibited, the ordinances in which this covenant is dispensed are the preaching

of the Word, and the administration of the sacraments of baptism and the Lord's Supper: which, though fewer in number, and
administered with more simplicity, and less outward glory, yet,
in them, it is held forth in more fullness, evidence and spiritual
efficacy, to all nations, both Jews and Gentiles.

This paradoxical relationship between the simplicity of worship after
the coming of Christ and the greater fullness of the gospel has challenged the church through the ages. The temptation is to think that the
greater reality of grace that comes through Christ is a reason to have
worship that is even more majestic and elaborate than that practiced
in the Old Testament temple. But the opposite is the case. Because of
the fuller revelation in Christ and the coming of the Holy Spirit, the
administration of the covenant of grace in the church depends less on
outward or external means than it did in Israel. Reformed worship
captured that important difference between the Old Testament saint's
desire for signs that would show God's power and the New Testament's abrogation of those old forms for the simpler means of grace
in the church.

When you throw in the doctrine of vocation and the priesthood
of all believers, you only add to the ways that Protestantism opened
up Christianity to accessible forms of worship and ordinary believers.
Protestants affirmed that simple people serve God in their everyday
duties and responsibilities as farmers, bakers, merchants, mothers,
and maids. No longer did a Christian need to go to a monastery or
nunnery to lead a life dedicated to God. Because creation was good,
because human beings were called to work in the created order as
part of God's provision for His creation, ordinary work in the world
was not evil. And when consecrated to God through prayer, this work
became a means of glorifying God even during the ordinary weekdays
in between the Lord's Days, the holy days set apart for public worship.

All these reforms, both in worship services proper and in the
workaday world of the common man and woman, point to the Reformation as a recovery of the ordinary. This does not mean that
Reformed Protestants are off the hook from charges of dullness or
that they may coast in their efforts to be faithful individually and

corporately. But even when Reformed Christians are doing their best to serve God and love their neighbors, they know that the authenticity and vigor of the Christian faith cannot be measured by outward displays of pomp, enthusiasm, and power. Protestants believe that after the epoch-making work of Christ, the surpassing glory of redemption cannot be contained in external or outward attempts at majesty or extraordinariness and that God uses foolish, weak, and ordinary means so that His people will boast only in Him and His power.

And don't ever forget that for all the beauty that Roman Catholics try to represent in their church buildings, they still fall short in the aesthetics sweepstakes when it comes to the music competition. Roman Catholics may have beautiful churches, basilicas, and cathedrals, but musically they struggle, as Thomas Day observes in his book *Why Catholics Can't Sing: The Culture of Catholicism and the Triumph of Bad Taste:*

> Somebody could write an inspirational book about people who used to convert to Catholicism because Gregorian chant first attracted them to the church. Each chapter would have the same outline: an individual who is not Catholic happens to visit a monastery or nunnery or seminary, is flabbergasted by the chant, and within a week asks to be received into the church.
>
> Somebody could write another book about individuals who lowered their estimation of Roman Catholicism because of the kind of music they heard recently in a monastery or nunnery or seminary. The atheist, for example, will look at a group of nuns floating from one "contemporary" song to another and instantly reach a verdict: "arrested adolescent development." The Protestant will observe seminarians trying to get everyone roused up with the exhilaration of the new Triumphalism and conclude: "the television evangelists can do this better." Even the devout member of the Roman Catholic laity will watch seminarians or monks or nuns wallowing in the goo of some "contemporary" song and quietly affirm: "Yes, this is where the church dumps its misfits."
>
> "Why is the church running out of priests and nuns?" There are hundreds of reasons and a small but significant one is

music. When it comes to music, all too often the seminaries, convents, and monasteries take careful aim and then deliberately shoot themselves in the foot. They deliberately promote music which has lots of sincerity but no crust, no grit, no credibility, no indication that it is wired directly to the deepest secrets of the universe. On a subconscious level, the music says that there is nothing special or distinctive or "heroic" about the religious life.[14]

No wonder architecture is important.

---

14. Thomas Day, *Why Catholics Can't Sing: The Culture of Catholicism and the Triumph of Bad Taste* (New York: Crossroad, 1990), 160–61.

9

IS PROTESTANTISM RESPONSIBLE FOR MODERNITY?

To hear some Christians who analyze culture talk, you would think that the fall of the human race did not occur in 4004 BC (using the dating techniques of Archbishop Ussher, who calculated biblical genealogies to arrive at the date of creation). For some, American society went into the gutter beginning in the 1960s when the sexual revolution challenged marital ties and personal chastity. That turning point in history led to a generation, the millennials, who "believe in nothing outside their own feelings, and cannot even make an argument for much of anything." What matters most is "what they feel." These young adults "are completely obsessed by material, sensate culture, and aspire to nothing higher than being comfortable, entertained, and happy."[1] For others, mainly Roman Catholics, the United States headed off the rails at the time of the American Revolution. "The First Amendment of the Constitution, in offering not 'articles of faith' but rather 'articles of peace,' secured religious freedom for Christians (and for others) while also respecting the rightful integrity of the secular."[2] The danger of the United States' political settlement is to deny theology and philosophy as proper grounds for the important contributions of religious freedom and the separation of church and

---

1. Rod Dreher, "Millennial Landslide," *Rod Dreher* (blog), *The American Conservative*, March 23, 2016, http://www.theamericanconservative.com/dreher/millennial-landslide-religion-secularism/.

2. Jeremy Beer, "Philosopher of Love," *The American Conservative* 12, no. 1 (January/February 2013), http://www.theamericanconservative.com/articles/philosopher-of-love-587/.

state. Without a proper philosophical basis, the political order of the United States cannot sustain itself; hence the sexual revolution of the 1960s was inevitable.

For still others—many traditionalist Roman Catholics—the West proceeded on a dangerous course of personal liberation and moral relativism with the launch of the Protestant Reformation. Brad Gregory's recent book on the Protestant Reformation attracted lots of readers and reactions because of his argument that Protestantism opened the floodgates of materialism, consumerism, and relativism after upending the stable truths and cultural order that Europe enjoyed through the blessings of Christendom. In *The Unintended Reformation*, Gregory attributes to Protestantism many of the woes of the modern world, especially the West's acquisitiveness, which he does not seem to notice was readily evident in the Renaissance popes who constructed the edifices and commissioned the artists whose labors attract tourists to Rome:

> Conflating prosperity with providence and opting for acquisitiveness as the lesser of two evils until greed was rechristened as benign self-interest, modern Christians have in effect been engaged in a centuries-long attempt to prove Jesus wrong. "You cannot serve both God and Mammon." Yes we can. Or so most participants in world history's most insatiably consumerist society, the United States, continue implicitly to claim through their actions, considering the number of self-identified American Christians in the early twenty-first century who seem bent on acquiring ever more and better stuff.[3]

These critiques of the modern West do not merely erroneously attribute to the medieval world a social order of harmony, love, justice, and—the favorite phrase of many anti-modernists—"human flourishing." These objections also involve the claim, sometimes explicit, that Roman Catholicism offers the best way to resist the modern world. In other words, as the author heard one participant at a conference

---

3. Brad S. Gregory, *The Unintended Reformation: How a Religious Revolution Secularized Society* (Cambridge, Mass.: Harvard University Press, 2012), 288.

of college students say, "The only way to be a true conservative is to be a Roman Catholic." This way of understanding the modern West generally associates democracy, capitalism, political liberty, freedom of conscience, and the separation of church and state—all departures from medieval Christendom—with Protestantism. It also regards Roman Catholicism as the only genuinely Christian way to resist the onslaught of the atheism and relativism so typical of the modern West.

As with most caricatures, a genuine likeness is present in both the depiction of Protestantism as an agent of modernity and Roman Catholicism as its fiercest foe in the modern West. But closer inspection also reveals that those who look to Rome as the place from which to resist the dangers of modern civilization ignore that Roman Catholicism's conservatism owed as much to historical circumstances as to divinely revealed truth. Conservatives who fault the Reformation for starting modernity's engine miss Protestantism's own capacity for conservative critique of modernity. In sum, Protestants have also resisted the modern world in a conservative fashion but without some of the folly that nineteenth-century popes exhibited. To be sure, many Protestants became caught up in the advances of the modern West as much as some Roman Catholics look nostalgically to the medieval past. But the genius of Protestantism has been a capacity to distinguish the affairs of this world from the coming of Christ's kingdom. That outlook has allowed Protestants to express a kind of conservatism that is not dependent on either clinging to the past or cheerleading for everything new. At its best, Protestantism remains committed to Christ, no matter what historical circumstances believers confront.

Protestants versus Roman Catholics Equals Liberty versus Tyranny?

In May of 1844 riots broke out in the neighborhood of Kensington, a small town that after 1852 would become a ward within the expanded boundaries of Philadelphia. The violence started when nativist Protestants assembled provocatively in an overwhelmingly Roman Catholic area. Nativists were part of the newly founded American Party, and they came to hear speeches against immigrants (like the Irish), the papacy, and Roman Catholicism. Party members suspected that the Vatican was planning to take over the United States and believed that Irish immigrants were the foot soldiers in papal strategy. The political platform of nativists included extending the period of naturalization to twenty-one years and limiting public office exclusively to native-born Americans.

The mix of nativists denouncing Irish Roman Catholics and Irish immigrants naturally defensive of their neighborhood, faith, and political status triggered violence. In a string of events that would resemble Belfast in the 1970s, skirmishes between nativist Protestants and Irish-American Roman Catholics broke into riots. In the first of three days of violence, one or two Protestants were killed by gunshots. The next day nativists returned and proceeded to burn down a city block full of homes, including a convent and a fire station. On the last day of rioting, Protestants escalated their attacks by burning down a Roman Catholic church, rectory, and female seminary. Within three days, fourteen people died, and the loss of property was the equivalent of almost four million dollars in today's value. Two months later, in the Southwark district outside Philadelphia, another riot broke out during Fourth of July celebrations in a predominantly Irish-American neighborhood. This time city officials and Roman Catholic authorities were armed, but that only meant more violence. After three days of fighting, which could only be contained by an estimated five thousand state militia, another fourteen residents had died and fifty were injured.

In addition to general suspicions of foreigners and specific animosities between the English and Irish, the Philadelphia riots were the result of the Roman Catholic bishop's objections to prayer and Bible reading in the city's public schools. Approximately six months before the riots, Francis Kenrick, Philadelphia's bishop, sent a letter to city controllers that took issue with the practice of beginning the school day with readings from the Protestant Bible. The Roman Catholic version of Scripture, the Douay translation, was based on the Vulgate and included the books of the Apocrypha. Roman Catholics

also objected to reading Scripture without comment or instruction. When city officials tried to mollify Roman Catholic objections,
nativist Protestants interpreted such policy as a threat to the nation's
political stability and character. Ever since the War for Independence
and debates over the Constitution, national leaders had argued that
virtue was necessary for the health of a free society and that the only
real source of virtue was religion. Because many of the founders
associated Roman Catholicism with bigotry, priestcraft, and supersti-
tion, the religion they preferred was some version of Protestantism.
That familiarity with Protestantism and the need for virtuous citizens
was partly responsible for the inclusion of prayer and Bible reading in public schools. In 1840s Philadelphia, Roman Catholics were
seemingly undermining the warm relationship between Christianity
and republicanism.

The 1844 riots were unusual, but the political character of anti-
Catholicism among American Protestants was not. In fact, until the
1960s, when the United States elected its first Roman Catholic president and Vatican II readjusted Roman Catholicism's posture toward
modern society, standard Protestant objections to Rome's followers
were not doctrinal but political. The worry for many Americans was
whether Roman Catholics could be good citizens in a free society
because of their loyalty to the papacy, a church officer who was not
simply the bishop with universal jurisdiction but also a prince who
ruled sovereignly over a territory on the Italian peninsula.

The riots in Philadelphia captured a much larger struggle in
which nineteenth-century Protestants and Roman Catholics seemed
to inhabit opposite sides of history. That century actually began eleven
years before 1800 with the American and French Revolutions, both
of which introduced political orders significantly different from
Christendom. Though for different reasons and in different ways, the
United States and France established governments independent of the
church (i.e., the separation of church and state). For some Protestants
in the United States, this new form of government, one that stressed
political freedom and opposed the tyranny of arbitrary or unchecked
rulers, was the culmination of the Reformation. Just as Martin Luther

had opposed the tyranny of the papacy, so the rise of political (classical) liberalism extended Protestantism's insights about ecclesiastical power to the monarchy and legislators. On the flip side, many Roman Catholics also regarded the American and French Revolutions as the culmination of the Reformation and as proof of the disrespect for authority and inherent social disorder that Protestants had introduced. To put it simply, Protestants tended to look at the novel conditions in the United States and France as welcome advances in the history of the West. Roman Catholics saw those same developments negatively, as declension from an ideal time when church, government, society, and culture coexisted harmoniously under the sacred canopy of Christian influence.

The most quoted founders of the United States—George Washington, Thomas Jefferson, John Adams, James Madison, and Benjamin Franklin—were sympathetic to Christianity but fearful of ecclesiastical power and dogmatism. They could often speak about the beauty and simplicity of the teachings of Jesus, whom they regarded as a supreme moral exemplar. For instance, Thomas Jefferson wrote in an 1822 letter to Benjamin Waterhouse that "the doctrines of Jesus are simple, and tend all to the happiness of man." The simple religion of Christianity involved belief in one perfect God and a future state of rewards and punishments and that the "sum of religion" was "to love God with all thy heart and thy neighbor as thyself." Support for Christian morality was especially important to the American founding because the nation's leaders understood that the only way to maintain a free society was through a virtuous people, and the only realistic way to cultivate virtue among the citizens was through Christianity. Even so, support for Christian ethics did not lead to support for churches or for theology. For instance, Benjamin Franklin wrote to his father in 1738, "I think vital religion has always suffered when orthodoxy is more regarded than virtue. The scriptures assure me that at the last day we shall not be examined on what we thought but what we did." In fact, the founders often blamed the churches for obscuring the plain teachings of Jesus through priestcraft, superstitious worship, and religious persecution. James Madison was typical. He held that ecclesiastical establishments were responsible for erecting "a spiritual tyranny on the ruins of the civil authority" and "upholding the thrones of political tyranny," in which case, not institutional religion but Christian morality was a valuable aid to republican government. The founders were especially suspicious of Roman Catholicism. Thomas Jefferson surmised in a letter from 1814 to Horatio Spafford that "in every country and in every age, the priest has been hostile to liberty." He added, the priest "is always in alliance with the despot." Meanwhile, in a letter to Jefferson, John Adams wondered, "Can a free government possibly exist with the Roman Catholic religion?"[4]

During the same era when the founders were attempting to reconcile Christianity with a new political order, the Vatican was experiencing firsthand the threats that republicanism and democracy posed to the ancient regime of Christendom. Unlike the revolution in North America, the French Revolution was decidedly anticlerical, and revolutionaries took out some of their grievances on Rome's bishops and priests. In the civil constitution of 1791, for example, the new government nationalized all monastic property and forbade monastic vows. It also required priests and bishops to take an oath of loyalty to the French nation and even forced some to marry. Pope Pius VI refused to allow the French priests and bishops to submit to the new laws. But this led to war between Napoleon and the pope and a French invasion of Rome. The papacy ceded more territories to the French government and paid millions of francs to reach a compromise. Even this did not stop Napoleon from taking Pius as a prisoner and escorting him into exile at Florence, outside Rome. Pius died while still a captive.

The affront of the French Revolution was largely responsible for the papacy's conservative posture from 1800 until 1950, though it had dug in its heels plenty of times since its explicit condemnation of Protestantism at Trent. In fact, throughout the period running up to the

---

4. Quotations compiled at "Faith of the Founding Fathers: Freedom from Religion, Disbelief in the Bible, Disdain for the Superstitions of Christianity," *The HyperTexts*, http://www.thehypertexts.com/Founding%20Fathers%20Faith%20Religion%20Bible %20Christianity%20God%20Jesus%20Quotes.htm.

Second Vatican Council, a series of popes condemned the conditions of liberal society that Protestants in the United States took for granted, such as the value of free inquiry, unrestricted markets, the separation of church and state, and popular sovereignty. The Syllabus of Errors (1864), issued by Pius IX in response to the further liberalization of European society, was a remarkable utterance of the papacy's anti-modernism. The list of condemned propositions totaled eighty and concluded with a point of general opposition to all modern developments. The Syllabus rejected the idea that the "Roman Pontiff can, and ought to, reconcile himself, and come to terms with progress, liberalism and modern civilization."[5] Of course the United States was a *novos ordo seclorum*, a new order for the ages, and clearly was an instance of modern political and economic arrangements. Did this mean that Roman Catholics in the United States should be opposed to their nation's modern political order?

What the Syllabus of Errors merely implied about American politics, Leo XIII made apparent (sort of) when he condemned Americanism as a heresy. *Testem Benevolentiae Nostrae* (1899), which formally condemned Americanism, came in response to the perception among European conservative Roman Catholics that clergy in the United States were guilty of adapting their faith and ministry to the norms of American society, either by embracing religious notions popular in the United States or by working to make ecclesiastical structures democratic. The papacy took another shot at American patterns of religious and political life in 1907, when Pius X condemned higher criticism and modernist theology in *Pascendi Dominici Gregis*. Although the encyclical was concerned more with deviations from Rome's understanding of Scripture and tradition, it connected deviations in theology to modern political trends, like the separation of church and state and freedom of conscience. The encyclical explained modernism's error this way:

---

5. "The Syllabus of Errors," no. 80, Papal Encyclicals Online, http://www .papalencyclicals.net/pius09/p9syll.htm.

Formerly it was possible to subordinate the temporal to the spiritual and to speak of some questions as mixed, conceding to the Church the position of queen and mistress in all such, because the Church was then regarded as having been instituted immediately by God as the author of the supernatural order. But this doctrine is today repudiated alike by philosophers and historians. The state must, therefore, be separated from the Church, and the Catholic from the citizen. Every Catholic, from the fact that he is also a citizen, has the right and the duty to work for the common good in the way he thinks best, without troubling himself about the authority of the Church, without paying any heed to its wishes, its counsels, its orders—nay, even in spite of its rebukes. (para. 24)

Whether Roman Catholics in the United States were guilty of Americanism or modernism, or whether the papacy had fairly represented the nature of American relations between church and state, the overwhelming tendency of popes after the French Revolution was to view democracy, republicanism, and religious toleration as deviations from Roman Catholic norms.

In the context of the American founding, which valued Christianity at least for its morality, and Rome's deep-seated opposition to modern political developments, Protestants in the United States developed a strain of anti-Catholicism that aimed almost exclusively at the political rather than the spiritual implications of Roman Catholicism. These Protestants regarded Roman Catholics not as wrong about the gospel but as political threats to the United States. Roman Catholic laity and clergy in America, the objection ran, were, first, subjects of a foreign prince, and, second, their Lord had repeatedly warned about the spiritual dangers of political systems like America's republican and liberal (in a nineteenth-century sense) form of government.

Presbyterians were hardly immune to the idea that Protestantism and political liberty went hand in hand or to the anti-Catholicism that accompanied such an understanding. At the time of the British colonists' War for Independence, John Witherspoon preached a sermon roughly a month before the signing of the Declaration of Independence that the Continental Congress circulated throughout the colonies. "The Dominion of Providence over the Passions of Men" gained a wide hearing because Witherspoon expressed the relationship between Christianity and political liberty in terms readily agreeable to many colonists. Although he exhorted Americans to behave virtuously if they were to obtain God's blessing, he had little trouble identifying the worthiness of their aims. "The cause in which America is now in arms," he declared, "is the cause of justice, of liberty, and of human nature." In fact, the desire for freedom stemmed from "a deep and general conviction" that religious and civil liberty, as well as "the temporal and eternal happiness of us and our society," depended on independence. "The knowledge of God and his truths," Witherspoon explained, "[has] from the beginning of the world been chiefly, if not entirely, confined to those parts of the earth, where some degree of liberty and political justice were to be seen." This was the logic that American Protestants took away from the War for Independence and carried with them in the establishment of the new nation: Protestant Christianity depended on civil magistrates, who protected civil liberties, and Protestantism itself was the source for the development of civil liberties. According to Witherspoon, "There is not a single instance in history in which civil liberty was lost, and religious liberty preserved entire."[6]

At the time of America's founding, Witherspoon was not worried much about Roman Catholicism since the Roman Church had roughly only thirty thousand church members in a nation of almost 3.5 million people. But when Roman Catholic immigrants began to establish a greater presence, Protestants turned their positive arguments about Protestantism and liberty into critiques of Rome's incompatibility with republicanism. During the 1830s and 1840s, the period of rioting in Philadelphia, Roman Catholics from Ireland and Germany began to arrive in the United States in unprecedented numbers. This demographic reality prompted Protestant spokesmen

---

6. John Witherspoon, "The Dominion of Providence over the Passions of Men," in Ellis Sandoz, ed., *Political Sermons of the American Founding Era, 1730-1805* (Indianapolis, Ind.: Liberty Fund, 1998), 1:549.

to apply Witherspoon's logic about republicanism and Protestantism to Roman Catholicism.

One of the first was Lyman Beecher, pastor at Park Street Congregational Church in Boston for many years before moving in 1832 to Cincinnati to preside over Lane Theological Seminary. From his vantage in Ohio, Beecher observed the arrival of Roman Catholic immigrants and fretted about the future of the country. His book *A Plea for the West* (1835) was a warning about the effects of the wrong religion on a republican form of government. On the one hand, Beecher affirmed that Roman Catholics' "civil and religious rights" should not be "abridged or violated." But, on the other hand, he believed that Rome's hierarchical structure and papal authority generated little plausibility for the form of government of the United States. To the notion that any religion was "just as good as another" for republican government, Beecher replied that Calvinism "had always been on the side of liberty in…struggles against arbitrary power." He explained: "Through the puritans, [Calvinism] breathed into the British constitution its most invaluable principles, and laid the foundations of the republican institutions of our nation, and felled the forests, and fought the colonial battles with Canadian Indians and French Catholics, when often our destiny balanced on a pivot and hung upon a hair." In fact, Beecher added, Calvinism "wept, and prayed, and fasted, and fought, and suffered through the revolutionary struggle, when there was almost no other creed…in the land."[7]

Aside from the historical record of Calvinist politics, Beecher was basically silent about Protestantism's direct links to liberty and democracy. Still, he believed that if Roman Catholics could adopt the forms of Protestant piety, they would become responsible citizens of the United States:

> If they associated with republicans, the power of caste would wear away. If they mingled in our schools, the republican atmosphere would impregnate their minds. If they scattered, unassociated, the attrition of circumstances would wear off

---

7. Lyman Beecher, *A Plea for the West* (Cincinnati: Truman and Smith, 1835), 80.

their predilictions and aversions. If they could read the Bible, and might and did, their darkened intellect would brighten, and their bowed down mind would rise. If they dared to think for themselves, the contrast of protestant independence with their thraldom, would awaken the desire of equal privileges, and put an end to an arbitrary clerical dominion over trembling super-stitious minds.[8]

Almost a half century after Beecher's *Plea for the West*, Josiah Strong, another Congregationalist minister, repeated the assump-tions that joined the cause of political liberty to the Protestant faith. A graduate of Lane Theological Seminary and a leading figure in the network of organizations that promoted the social gospel, Strong identified immigration, Roman Catholicism, Mormonism, intem-perance, socialism, wealth, and urbanization as the seven perils threatening religious and political liberty in the United States in his popular book *Our Country: Its Possible Future and Its Present Crisis* (1885). His solution to these social ills was to convince Anglo-Saxon Americans of their "commanding influence in the world's future" and their need to choose the spiritual and Christian course instead of a materialistic and atheistic one.

As with Beecher, Strong's objections to Roman Catholicism stemmed much more from political and cultural assumptions than from doctrinal convictions. In his chapter "Romanism," Strong out-lined the basic antagonism between "the fundamental principles of our government" and "those of the Catholic church." He found numerous statements by popes and from the Curia in opposition to freedom of conscience, public schools, and the separation of church and state. Like Beecher, Strong believed that civil liberty was inherent to Protestantism. The two greatest characteristics of Anglo-Saxons were political freedom and spiritual Christianity, thus explaining why the English, the British colonists, and the people of the United States were both the freest and the most devout. "It is not necessary to argue," Strong wrote, "to those for whom I write that the two great

---

8. Beecher, *Plea for the West*, 80.

needs of mankind, that all men may be lifted up into the light of the highest Christian civilization, are, first, a pure, spiritual Christianity, and, second, civil liberty."[9] Such confidence may have made complete sense to Strong's Anglo-American Protestant readers. And it clearly reflected the older political and religious calculus of Christian republicanism. But it hardly explained the precise relationship between Protestant devotion and political liberty. Even so, assumptions that Protestantism guaranteed America's political institutions and ideals were sufficiently influential to make Strong's book a best seller.

These are only a few examples of American reflection on the relationship between Western Christianity's two branches and the fortunes of the United States. But they do reflect the general point—namely, that Protestantism and republicanism were at least compatible, if not downright mutually reinforcing, and that Roman Catholicism clung to an older political order that republics like the United States overthrew. As a result, American Protestants developed a strain of anti-Catholicism that was largely political along with a form of patriotism that unhealthily equated the faith with democracy and liberty. The outcome was an assumption that Protestants were invariably on the side of social progress, from the Dark Ages to modern enlightenment, and that Roman Catholics were conservative, superstitious, bigoted, and backward. This also means invariably that if an American believer wants to dissent from the logic and momentum of progressive politics, from abolitionism to abortion rights, he or she finds more resources for political conservatism in Roman Catholic sources. Since popes opposed unchecked support for equality and freedom, Roman Catholic theologians, clergy, and laity usually thought critically about political liberalism in ways that escaped rank-and-file Protestants. Hence, some can look at the past and conclude that to be a true political conservative means becoming Roman Catholic.

---

9. Josiah Strong, *Our Country: Its Possible Future and Its Present Crisis* (New York: Baker & Taylor, 1885), 47, 49.

Protestant Anti-Modernism

Anyone who knows the history of Protestantism also understands that a progressive view of history that runs from the Dark Ages to the enlightened modern age received criticism from significant Protestant theologians and church leaders. After all, the execution of the heretic Michael Servetus did not happen in a Roman Catholic nation but in John Calvin's Geneva. That example is one indication that Protestantism was not synonymous with an overly expansive idea of freedom, diversity, or tolerance. English Protestants who drew much inspiration from Calvin—namely, the Puritans—also established a colony in North America where, in some cases, civil law came directly from Old Testament legal codes and prohibited non-Puritans from practicing their own faith. That explains why Massachusetts authorities banned Roger Williams, who founded a rival colony, Rhode Island, which implemented the separation of church and state. In the nineteenth century, even after the coming of classical liberal politics in the form of the U.S. Constitution, Presbyterians, who were among the strongest Calvinists, defended slavery not simply on the grounds that the Bible did not condemn the institution but also out of a significant critique of egalitarian ideals and radical individualism that could undermine the authority of all hierarchies, including pastors, parents, and teachers. At the end of that same century, Dutch Calvinists under the leadership of Abraham Kuyper formed a political party, the Anti-Revolution Party, dedicated to opposing the supposed radical politics of the French Revolution. Kuyper believed that the basic principles of the French Revolution were an assault on family, church, and school unless they were hemmed in by policies recognizing the importance of social institutions that mediated between the citizen and the state.

Today's Protestants, even theologically conservative ones, are naturally uncomfortable with many of these aspects of anti-modern Protestantism. Few believe that heresy qualifies as a capital offense or that slavery is anything other than a gross perversion of legitimate social relations between employers and workers. The point here is not to bless anti-modern Protestantism. It is rather to remind Protestants and Roman Catholics that the Reformation itself was nearly as much a part of a pre-modern, pre-democratic, pre-liberal, pre-egalitarian world as was the medieval church. It is also to remind both groups that Protestants voiced as many objections to the rise of modern society as Roman Catholics. The popes may have given the modern Roman Catholic Church a body of texts to categorize as social teaching. But Protestants could match such teaching pound for pound. Consider the reflections of the Westminster Assembly in the Larger Catechism, question 142, on the implications of the eighth commandment ("Thou shalt not steal"):

> The sins forbidden in the eighth commandment, besides the neglect of the duties required, are, theft, robbery, man-stealing, and receiving anything that is stolen; fraudulent dealing, false weights and measures, removing landmarks, injustice and unfaithfulness in contracts between man and man, or in matters of trust; oppression, extortion, usury, bribery, vexatious lawsuits, unjust enclosures and depredation; engrossing commodities to enhance the price; unlawful callings, and all other unjust or sinful ways of taking or withholding from our neighbor what belongs to him, or of enriching ourselves; covetousness; inordinate prizing and affecting worldly goods; distrustful and distracting cares and studies in getting, keeping, and using them; envying at the prosperity of others; as likewise idleness, prodigality, wasteful gaming; and all other ways whereby we do unduly prejudice our own outward estate, and defrauding ourselves of the due use and comfort of that estate which God hath given us.

If Protestants no longer share the politics of their forefathers in the faith, the reason is likely similar to the ones that drove modern Roman Catholics to abandon medieval views about the separation of church and state—that is, that the pope is above the state and the magistrate's authority comes only through the church.

Just as important for understanding Protestantism and modernity is the profound critique of modernism that Protestant theologians registered against Christian efforts to adapt the faith to the modern world. Indeed, one of the greatest developments in Christian circles after the Civil War was a sense that many of the older truths of Scripture and theology were no longer relevant for the demands of a modernizing society, one in which industries and cities expanded and economic and political developments required experts trained not in morality or theology but in the specific academic disciplines available at research universities. Protestant modernists in the late nineteenth century gazed at the changes of modern society and understood that the way the church had been doing ministry was not going to keep pace. They even looked at economic, political, and academic progress as signs of the coming of God's kingdom. Some Roman Catholic theologians in North America and Europe also looked at the advances in human knowledge and changes in politics and economics and argued that the church needed to adapt. In 1899 Pope Leo XIII responded to bishops in the United States who wanted the church to become more American by condemning "Americanism" as a heresy. His successor, Pius X, went a step further and in 1907 condemned modernism. In his encyclical *Pascendi Dominici Gregis*, Pius asserted that among modernists' many errors was that they "do not deny but actually admit, some confusedly, others in the most open manner, that all religions are true." Both popes understood the process of cutting and pasting ancient and timeless truths to modern circumstances was to deny truth altogether.

That was the same position that Protestants like J. Gresham Machen took. The professor of New Testament at Princeton Seminary stood in a tradition of conservative Presbyterian dissent from the assured conclusions that modern science provided clear insight into the meaning of Scripture. In 1923, during the peak years of debate in the so-called fundamentalist controversy, Machen wrote *Christianity and Liberalism* to argue that Protestant modernism was an entirely different religion from historic Christianity. The reason had to do with the way in which Protestants had adapted settled truths to the realities of modern life (social and intellectual):

> Admitting that scientific objections may arise against the particularities of the Christian religion—against the Christian doctrines of the person of Christ, and of redemption through

His death and resurrection—the liberal theologian seeks to rescue certain of the general principles of religion, of which these particularities are thought to be mere temporary symbols, and these general principles he regards as constituting "the essence of Christianity." It may well be questioned, however, whether this method of defense will really prove to be efficacious; for...what the liberal theologian has retained after abandoning to the enemy one Christian doctrine after another is not Christianity at all, but a religion which is so entirely different from Christianity.[10]

Machen's anti-modernism did not include opposition to political and social developments since 1789. Although he was suspicious of modern forms of urbanization and industrialism, not to mention Progressive politics, Machen was a libertarian who lauded the American founding and even defended the freedom of Roman Catholics to proselytize and form parochial schools. In other words, Machen's anti-modernism neither committed him to a prerevolutionary (or feudal) social order nor to an embrace of democracy and freedom as the outworking of biblical principles. Some forms of Protestant anti-modernism, like Machen's, were fundamentally about preserving the faith while regarding social and political life as matters indifferent because they were not clearly taught in Scripture.

For Roman Catholics, separating faith and society is a much more difficult task than for Protestants since the papacy and its political claims were so connected to a social order that the French and American Revolutions (in different degrees) overturned. For good reason Protestants recognize Roman Catholic critiques of modernity's extremes as insightful. But the overlap between Roman Catholic and Protestant political critiques has less to do with dogma or biblical teaching than with prudential assessments of social order and political stability, two arenas of reflection that admit a variety of perspectives. At the same time, while Protestants and Roman Catholics

---

10. J. Gresham Machen, *Christianity and Liberalism* (New York: Macmillan, 1923), 6.

have opposed theological modernity, they have done so for reasons internal to their respective traditions—namely, conflicts with either the churches' confessions or magisterium's teaching. Either way, Protestants have a tradition of criticizing modernity that rivals Roman Catholicism's. In fact, some Protestants have remained more critical of modernism than Roman Catholics, the subject of the final chapter.

10

WHAT IF AT VATICAN II ROME ABANDONED BEING THE CHURCH JESUS FOUNDED?

Contemporary Roman Catholicism is incoherent if not schizophrenic. On the one hand, apologists and converts look to Rome as the ballast against relativism and uncertainty that modern life throws at Christians. On the other hand, defenders of Roman Catholicism point to the church's capacity to adapt, shift, even change—the preferred word is *develop*—and so avoid the strictures and mentality of Protestant fundamentalism. That contradictory view is not something that onlookers need to work hard to find. The idea that Rome is both rock solid and ever fluid is part and parcel of contemporary Roman Catholic discussion. Bishops do nothing to prevent such contradictory ideas. For some reason, Protestants who convert to Rome never seem to be troubled by the evasiveness of Roman Catholic claims. Apparently, you go to Rome for stability and answers and then ignore how diverse the voices are and how many different responses your questions receive. All this is supposedly not a bug but a feature.

Dwight Longenecker, a graduate of Bob Jones University who became Anglican and then converted to Roman Catholicism, explained that much of the appeal of Rome is its stand for objective truth. He admitted that the Church of England's liturgy and tradition was a tonic that countered Low-Church Protestantism's bare-bones atmosphere. But the average Anglican priest relied much more on pragmatic considerations than theology when determining the best course for his ministry to his parishioners. Anglicanism was not really a church but a collection of "clubs, confraternities, associations, and societies." The reason was that Anglicanism had "no objective theology." "Everything from choice of liturgy to the most crucial questions of sacramental practice and moral theology were made on relativistic principles," Longenecker complained. Pragmatism was precisely what enabled Anglo-Catholics and Low-Church Anglican evangelicals to exist in the same communion. Both camps have "relativism at the foundation of their theological method."[1] In such a context, theology is only metaphorical, doctrine merely a poem. In Rome Longenecker found the remedy for Anglicanism's weak grip on truth. Not only did Pope John Paul II affirm and defend objective truth over against postmodern relativism in his encyclical *Fides et Ratio* but he also identified the conditions that made objective truth possible. Perhaps a bit self-serving and guilty of circular reasoning to boot, John Paul II's conditions included authority—specifically, a church office that was objective, historical, universal, scriptural, and divinely appointed. Those marks of objective truth pointed directly at the papacy, so the bishop of Rome became for Longenecker the monument of objective truth with the only means capable of withstanding modern skepticism.

Readers of this priest's defense of truth and the papacy will no doubt scratch their heads when they turn to other Roman Catholic literature on the nature of the church and its devotion. Evyatar Marienberg, a professor of religious studies at University of North Carolina Chapel Hill, presents a different side of Roman Catholicism in his book *Catholicism Today: An Introduction to the Contemporary Catholic Church*. In his first chapter, "Being Catholic," Marienberg stresses the feature that drove Longenecker from the Church of England to Rome. Due to its size, history, and cultural diversity, Marienberg writes, Roman Catholicism "can generally be characterized, especially today, as inclusive and compromising." "Contradictory inclinations and views exist side by side and in relative peace within Catholicism's walls," he writes. Rome's ability to compromise stems

---

1. Dwight Longenecker, "House of Mirrors: Relativity and Anglican Comprehensiveness," in Dwight Longenecker, ed., *The Path to Rome: Modern Journeys to the Catholic Church* (Leominster, England: Gracewing, 1999), 36, 39.

from its "inherent flexibility."[2] Later in the book, when Marienberg describes Roman Catholic dogma—the teaching "deemed essential by the supreme hierarchy of the Church"—he admits that portions of the church "may relate to these same doctrines differently." This means that large numbers of Roman Catholics "have difficulty accepting" the doctrine that the bread and wine in the Mass become the actual body and blood of Christ, as well as the doctrines of Christ's resurrection and the immaculate conception of Mary. In fact, the gap between what the church teaches and what church members believe is "at times very large."[3] Marienberg does not mention but could include the wide distance between his and Longenecker's depiction of Roman Catholicism. Readers could legitimately wonder if the way that Roman Catholics tolerate such diversity is all that different from the variations that characterize the Church of England. Longenecker may counter that at least Rome has a bishop to uphold and defend the truth—the papacy—with universal jurisdiction. But then comes the question of why the papacy does not prevent the same kind of diversity and relativism that exists among Anglicans.

Roman Catholic diversity only highlights the weakness rather than the authority of the papacy and raises the question, What happened? To be sure, when Pope Pius IX issued the Syllabus of Errors (1864), Roman Catholicism was more like the church that Longenecker thought he was joining. But over time, Rome became Marienberg's "Catholicism today," which accepts if not celebrates variety and inclusiveness. What happened, many argue, was the Second Vatican Council. During that pivotal decade when the West was questioning and overturning inherited social and moral norms, the cardinals and bishops of the Roman Catholic Church decided to open up their communion to the modern world. Previously, Pius IX had condemned any effort to accommodate modern developments. One hundred years later, the Second Vatican Council gave up such

2. Evyatar Marienberg, *Catholicism Today: An Introduction to the Contemporary Catholic Church* (New York: Routledge, 2015), 22.

3. Marienberg, *Catholicism Today*, 47.

opposition. Now the church would come alongside the modern world because the wider society was not nearly as bad or as dangerous as previous popes, at least since the Council of Trent but especially since the French Revolution, had thought.

What Happened at Vatican II?

To understand how Roman Catholicism became infected with the same spirit that afflicted Protestantism modernism—namely, a desire to adapt to and accommodate contemporary life—requires a brief overview of the Council of bishops and cardinals that met periodically in Rome between 1962 and 1965. Interpretations vary as much as interpreters who line up to assess the council. Even Pope Benedict XVI spoke of a hermeneutic of continuity, one that interpreted the council's statements in the light of the church's existing doctrine and practice, in contrast to a hermeneutic of discontinuity, one that saw the Second Vatican Council as a break from the past.[4] No one can admit that Roman Catholicism changed at Vatican II. To make that concession would mean that truth and faith, which are supposed to transcend historical flux, are as much a part of historical development as any other part of human life. It would also mean that the church had erred in the past, and now, with Vatican II, Rome was correcting its errors, an impossibility if you think that the magisterium, the teaching authority of the church, is infallible. All this suggests that the council is one of the epoch-making events in Roman Catholic history, one fraught with dangers to those who locate the church's glory days in the era of medieval Christendom. Complicating interpretations of the council even more is that when Pope John XXIII called the council, he had no error or threat in mind for bishops to consider. The church faced no obvious crisis. Instead, John XXIII wanted the council to update Roman Catholicism for the sake of its own spiritual vitality, Christian unity, and world peace. Hindsight

---

4. See "Address of His Holiness Benedict XVI to the Roman Curia Offering Them His Christmas Greetings, 22 December 2005," The Holy See, http://w2.vatican.va/content/benedict-xvi/en/speeches/2005/december/documents/hf_ben_xvi_spe_20051222_roman-curia.html.

makes it easy to notice the effects of two world wars, the effort to rebuild Europe, and the uncertainty of the Cold War on church officials who wanted Roman Catholicism to reposition itself at the center of European recovery and global politics.

Another factor in assessing the council's significance is the relative authority of the documents it produced. In total, the cardinals and bishops produced sixteen statements. The most authoritative were the four constitutions that covered ecclesiology, the church in the modern world, revelation, and liturgy. Constitutions technically pertain to doctrinal matters and therefore go to the essence of the church's teaching. The other twelve statements were either decrees or declarations that addressed practical or pastoral matters. The authority of these statements depends, as one theologian explains, on a set of factors. Did the document come from the pope with the support of the council? Was the statement representative of legitimate interests in the church? Did the statement capture the best reflection on the subject at the time? And how has the statement been received by the church's theologians? According to these criteria, the most important statements of the Council were seven of the sixteen total: the Dogmatic Constitution of the Church, the Pastoral Constitution on the Church in the Modern World, the Decree on Ecumenism, the Constitution on Sacred Liturgy, the Dogmatic Constitution on Divine Revelation, the Declaration on Religious Freedom, and the Declaration on the Relationship of the Church to Non-Christian Religions.

The council introduced changes that from one angle looked like the sort of reforms that Protestants had advocated four centuries earlier. For instance, in its Constitution on Sacred Liturgy, the council insisted that worship needed to be understood if it was to be effective in conveying grace. Liturgy needed to be accessible to the people. This meant that worship needed to be in the vernacular language of the worshipers. Also, in the Dogmatic Constitution on Divine Revelation, the council showed greater flexibility in its attachment to tradition in relationship to Scripture. The Word of God was supreme, and the teaching authority of the church, according to the council, "is not above the word of God, but serves it."[5] Although the teaching of the authority of the church was still crucial, the council also affirmed that Scripture and tradition were "so linked and joined together that one cannot stand without the others" and that all sources of truth depended on the illumination of the Holy Spirit. The council also recognized more than previously the value and contribution of the laity as opposed to stressing the hierarchy in understanding the nature and work of the church. As such, the Decree on the Apostolate of the Laity included laypeople in the mission of the church as part of Christ's commission to His apostles.[6] That is almost the priesthood of all believers.

Although these adjustments seemed to move Rome away from a hierarchical and authoritarian church toward one accessible to the laity and flexible in its ministry, the council went even further by appearing to be open to truths and believers who were not Roman Catholic. In its Declaration on the Relationship of the Church to Non-Christian Religions, the council recognized "the ray of truth" that enlightened all the world's faiths and encouraged dialogue and collaboration with non-Christian religions, especially Judaism. In the Decree on Ecumenism, the church recognized that Rome shared with Protestants the same Scripture, the same life of grace, the same virtues (faith, hope, and charity), the same Spirit, and the same baptism. As such, the council committed Rome to a path of restoring unity among Western Christians, not the *return* of Protestants to Rome. The council even conceded that Rome was to blame, along with Protestantism, for the division of the church at the Reformation. This openness to other religions and to Protestantism bore further fruit in the council's Declaration on Religious Freedom, what was arguably the most controversial of the proceeding's final outcomes. Rather than upholding its earlier position that in politics "error has no rights," the idea that the state should not tolerate false or erroneous religious views,

---

5. Here I rely on the summary of Richard McBrien, *Catholicism* (San Francisco: Harper, 1994), 675.

6. McBrien, *Catholicism*, 676, 678.

the council went on record in support of freedom for all beliefs, even those considered to be wrong. It condemned coercion of belief in all forms and all penalties that impeded religious practice.

After having opposed, at least formally, most aspects of modern society since the Reformation, the Second Vatican Council looked to insiders like an ecclesiastical revolution, comparable to the Reformation's upheaval. The fiftieth anniversary of the Council paved the way for Roman Catholics who were young during the 1960s to reflect as seniors on the significance of Vatican II. James Carroll remembered fondly the approval that the Council seemed to give to the youth's desire to fight injustice: "What set us young Catholics apart from others of the 1960's generation," Carroll wrote for the *Boston Globe*, "is that we had been conscripted into the era's revolution not against authority, but by authority. Vatican II dared us to change, and we did.... Instead of mindless subservience, we took initiatives, reinventing the liturgy, throwing ourselves into anti-poverty work, and recognizing Jesus on the bread line." When John Paul II started to put a brake on change, the 1960s generation became frustrated with the hierarchy's conservatism. But Carroll knew that the genie could not go back in the bottle. With liberty of conscience now the norm, Roman Catholics "began claiming their own religious liberty, at times rejecting the authority of popes and bishops—and still going to Communion."[7]

John O'Malley, an accomplished historian who wrote an important book on the council also wrote for the *New York Times* about the revolutionary way in which Vatican II opened the door for Roman Catholics to change their understanding of other faiths. Before the council, O'Malley recalled, Roman Catholics "were not only forbidden to pray with those of other faiths but also indoctrinated into a disdain or even contempt for them." But now, "for the first time, Catholics were encouraged to foster friendly relations with Orthodox and

---

7. James Carroll, "The Catholic Church's Lost Revolution," *Boston Globe*, September 30, 2012, https://www.bostonglobe.com/opinion/2012/09/29/vatican-the-catholic -church-lost-revolution/SBwSGcAoMYGtPfIB5DCWzN/story.html.

Protestant Christians, as well as Jews and Muslims, and even to pray
with them." In O'Malley's experience as a Jesuit priest, such openness
led not just to interreligious dialogue but also to interfaith ceremonies. He admitted, "I have officiated at weddings alongside rabbis and
Methodist pastors." Meanwhile, Roman Catholic colleges and universities "now as a matter of course have rabbis, imams and Protestant
ministers on their campus ministry staff."[8] As lax as some evangelical
colleges may be, the thought of a Wheaton or a Westmont including
Muslims and Jews as part of their chapel program is unimaginable
(for now).

At the same time, Vatican II changed the average Roman Catholic's participation in worship and, in hindsight, not for the better. Ken
Woodward, longtime religion reporter for *Newsweek*, remembered
not so fondly the introduction of the Mass in English:

> At its inception it was better described, as one forgotten wit
> put it, as "the participation of the laity in the confusion of the
> clergy." Compared to the old Latin liturgy, I found the new
> version about as moving as a freight train. Silence was now a
> liturgical vice, conscripted congregational responses the new
> regimen of worship. In a pale imitation of the early Christians'
> kiss of peace, there was now a scripted pause.... In place of my
> much-loved Latin hymns and chants, the new liturgists bade us
> sing old Reformation anthems like Martin Luther's "A Mighty
> Fortress Is Our God." I could not bring myself to join in when
> the chosen hymn was "Amazing Grace"—in fact, I still refuse to
> do so. It's a lovely piece, all about getting one's self individually
> saved, Evangelical-style, but theologically it has no place in the
> corporate worship of the Catholic Church.
>
> What the liturgists didn't borrow from Protestant hymnals,
> they conjured up by themselves. Mostly, it was folk music sung
> to plucked guitars with relentlessly upbeat lyrics about how
> much a nice God loves us and aren't we fortunate to be his cho-

---

8. John W. O'Malley, "Opening the Church to the World," *New York Times*, Octo-
ber 10, 2012, http://www.nytimes.com/2012/10/11/opinion/vatican-ii-opened-the
-church-to-the-world.html.

sen people. There was no awe, no hint of the biblical fear of the Lord in this music, only the mild diuretic of self-congratulation.[9]

Many priests and theologians would likely have disagreed with Woodward's interpretation of the council's significance for the church, but the numbers suggest the journalist had a better read of the church than many officers. Woodward concluded that Vatican II had failed "to pass on the faith, through the liturgy or through the classroom." The effect was to "snip two generations of young Catholics from their own religious roots." The decline in Roman Catholics entering religious orders already mentioned in chapter 5 deserves amplification for anyone trying to assess the significance of Vatican II. Between 1965 and 2016, the number of priests in the United States went from just under 59,000 to just over 37,000. During the same period the number of seminarians declined from around 8,300 to roughly 3,500. In the five decades after Vatican II, the number of parishes in the United States has decreased by almost 400, from roughly 17,600 to 17,200, figures that do not reveal that the number of parishes grew to a high of 19,600 in 1990. During the same time, the number of parishes without priests has grown from roughly 550 to 3,500. Defenders of Rome may take comfort from growth in the number of Roman Catholics from 46.3 million in 1965 to 67.7 million in 2016. But that increase is certainly not the result of converts since someone is simply born and baptized into the church and the hierarchy is loathe to execute church discipline or purge church rolls of inactive church members. As this is the case, a better indication of Roman Catholic vigor may be the number of church members who choose to enter religious orders or the priesthood. At the same time, the number of baptisms—from 1.3 million in 1965 to 670,000 in 2016—is indicative of a decline among church members despite an increase on church

---

9. Kenneth L. Woodward, "Reflections on the Revolution in Rome: Reporting the Catholic Sixties," *First Things*, February 2013, https://www.firstthings.com/article/2013/02/reflections-on-the-revolution-in-rome.

rolls. At the same time, attendance at Mass has gone from 55 percent to 22 percent during the fifty years after Vatican II.[10]

A Roman Catholic writer, R. Jared Staudt, finds the statistical revelations even more disconcerting than simply the significance of numerical loss. The small number of Roman Catholics who go to confession actually indicates something woeful about the people who do go to Mass. (It also says something significant about priests and bishops who read these statistics and articles and seemingly do little to shepherd their flocks.) Staudt observes:

> When we speak of mercy, it has to begin in the Confession, with the sacrament that Christ gave us to bestow his mercy on us. When we look at the numbers, it appears that Catholics are rejecting or are simply unconcerned about receiving God's mercy. A report from CARA, Georgetown's Center for Applied Research in the Apostolate, conducted almost a decade ago shows that "three-quarters of Catholics report that they never participate in the sacrament of Reconciliation or that they do so less than once a year." Frankly, this statistic alone demonstrates the heart of the spiritual crisis facing the Church. The Church has been given the enormous grace by Christ to forgive sins, but people just aren't very interested.

It gets worse when you do the math of those who take Communion unworthily:

> How do we know we are receiving the Lord unworthily? First... an overwhelming majority of Catholics do not receive the sacrament of Reconciliation. Second, add to that regular Mass attendance for Catholics is only about 22 percent (once again, according to CARA). Catholics are not fulfilling the precepts of the Church to attend Mass on Sunday and Holy Days and to confess their sins. This means that many Catholics presenting themselves to receive Communion are not in the state of grace.[11]

10. "Frequently Requested Church Statistics," Center for Applied Research in the Apostolate, http://cara.georgetown.edu/frequently-requested-church-statistics.

11. R. Jared Staudt, "The Spiritual Roots of the Church's Crisis," *Crisis Maga-*

How many times can Roman Catholics assert that Rome is the church Christ founded, hoping to soften the blow of these revelations about the spiritual health of Roman Catholicism? Do those Protestants who convert to Rome think the disparity between faith and practice counts for nothing?

Protestants who go to Rome may also want to reflect on the second generation of Roman Catholics who grew up never having known the pre–Vatican II church. Here the fascinating and sobering sociological investigation by Christian Smith is revealing. It is also poignant since Smith is a former evangelical who converted to Roman Catholicism and does not allow the poor spiritual health of Roman Catholics to dampen his esteem for Rome over Protestantism. Here is how one set of sociologists summarized Smith's findings in *Young Catholic America: Adults In, Out of, and Gone from the Church* (2014):

> According to Smith and his colleagues, "compared both to official Catholic norms of faithfulness and to other types of Christian teens in the United States [especially young Mormons and young evangelical Protestants], contemporary U.S. Catholic teens are faring rather badly," "show up as fairly weak" and reflect "the relative religious laxity of their parents."
>
> Finding more continuity than change in young Catholics' religiosity as they become young adults, Smith and his colleagues say that the "crucial factor" has been "the inability and sometimes unwillingness of a critical mass of the parents of the Catholic and ex-Catholic emerging adults we studied—and those half a generation earlier—to model, teach, and pass on the faith to their children."
>
> In the Smith team's view, the low religiosity scores of young Catholics are traceable to the low levels of religiosity among their parents, who have failed to produce the high levels of

compliance found in Protestant sects, the Church of Jesus Christ of Latter-day Saints, and the pre-Vatican II Catholic church.[12]

This is certainly an indictment of the post–Vatican II world, but these Roman Catholic sociologists believe Smith is looking at a glass only half full. Smith is guilty, they write, of using "a view of Catholicism as essentially a compliance-based religion." He expects church members to "agree with the creeds and code of conduct that have been formulated by religious authorities over time." In other words, Smith uses pre–Vatican II Roman Catholicism as a benchmark for evaluating the post–Vatican II church, a starting point that makes perfect sense if you think that Rome is the church that Jesus founded. Why would you ever want to alter what Jesus instituted? But such a mind-set fosters "an either/or, small-tent view of Catholicism."[13]

What the sociological critics of Smith propose instead is a "conscience-centered" understanding of Roman Catholicism that breaks with a "compliance-based" model. These sociologists take their cue from the changes that Vatican II introduced when it affirmed freedom of conscience:

> Our studies show that pre-Vatican II Catholics learned a compliance-oriented approach that emphasized the teaching authority of the clergy, demanded strict adherence to all official church teachings, and often relied on fear and guilt to produce record-high levels of conformity.
>
> Then, as a result of changes in American society and changes in the Catholic church, everything changed. Pre-Vatican II Catholics' best efforts to pass their compliance-centered understanding of the faith on to their children were often mitigated by the cultural revolution of the 1960s and the implementation of Vatican II, both of which fostered a more personal approach to religion.

---

12. William V. D'Antonio, James D. Davidson, Mary L. Gautier, and Katherine Meyer, "Assumptions in Study on Young Catholics Lead to Unnecessarily Grim Outlook," *National Catholic Reporter*, December 6, 2014, https://www.ncronline.org /news/people/assumptions-study-young-catholics-lead-unnecessarily-grim-outlook.

13. D'Antonio et al., "Assumptions in Study on Young Catholics."

The three most recent generations learned a more conscience-centered approach that emphasizes Catholics' responsibility for their own faith, including their responsibility to inform their own consciences, and to follow them as much as possible, even if this involves disagreement with church teachings.

These macro-level changes produced generational differences within Catholic families. The largest disjuncture is between pre-Vatican II parents, who remain the most loyal and active generation, and their Vatican II, post-Vatican II and millennial offspring, who have embraced the more individualistic, conscience-oriented understanding of the church.[14]

Either way, Smith and his critics recognize that something fundamentally changed with Vatican II. Some Roman Catholics celebrate that change, and some regret it. But such alterations raise serious questions about how conservative or liberal Rome is and should pose challenges to any Protestant who thinks she is joining the church in which Augustine bore his soul or Thomas Aquinas formulated his propositions. They are going to encounter a church much closer to mainline Protestantism, where doctrines are simply indications of an earlier generation's attempt to formulate religious mysteries and personal preferences rule under the heading of freedom of conscience. And though Roman Catholics still differ from mainline Protestants on sex and women's ordination, that does not prevent many church members from ignoring church teaching that regards contraception as a mortal sin or keep bishops and cardinals (and even popes) from wanting to revise Rome's understanding of adultery and divorce.[15]

One statistical area in which Roman Catholics might take comfort is education. The parochial school, once the bedrock of showing your religious bona fides in the United States, is showing the same signs of decline as parish life. Between 1965 and 2016, primary-age

---

14. D'Antonio et al., "Assumptions in Study on Young Catholics."

15. For a conservative critique of the recent synods on marriage and Pope Francis's ensuing encyclical, see Richard A. Spinello, "*Amoris Laetitia* and the Post-Modern Papacy of Pope Francis," *Crisis Magazine*, January 24, 2017, http://www.crisis magazine.com/2017/amoris-laetitia-post-modern-papacy-pope-francis.

school children enrolled in parochial schools have declined from 3.4 million to 2.5 million. The loss for high-school-aged teens is even more pronounced, from 1.3 million to roughly 600,000. But students in Roman Catholic colleges and universities have resisted trends in the larger U.S. church. In 1965, a little over 400,000 Roman Catholic students attended church institutions of higher education. By 2016 that number had increased to roughly 775,000.

Before any Roman Catholic apologist takes heart from these numbers, he likely needs to remember Christian Smith's findings about the church's teenagers and the sort of Roman Catholic universities that educate them. Roman Catholic institutions of higher education may be growing numerically, but in so doing they may also be becoming indistinguishable from secular or liberal colleges and universities. Consider the recent case of Providence College, where its popular professor of literature, Anthony Esolen, objected to the way the current concept of diversity undermines serious study. The professor wrote articles critical of students' demands for greater sensitivity to race and gender in the classroom and heard in response charges of racism. Esolen tried to meet with students, but they refused. The students did meet with Providence's president, Brian Shanley, who weakly defended Esolen's right to academic freedom but criticized the professor for causing pain. As writers for the conservative publication *Crisis Magazine* put it: "And what is charitable about a Catholic college's abandonment of a Catholic professor for expressing his Catholic beliefs? Shanley is clearly grieved that Esolen is protected by those uncharitable concepts of academic freedom and freedom of speech. 'He certainly does not speak for me,' Shanley intoned, eager to avoid association with a man who speaks truth that irritates the mob."[16] The opposition Esolen faced at Providence provoked him to go to Thomas More College, a small traditionalist Roman Catholic school in New Hampshire that is explicitly independent of bishops

---

16. Emmett McGroarty and Jane Robbins, "The Providence College Mob Comes for Anthony Esolen," *Crisis Magazine*, December 2, 2016, http://www.crisis magazine.com/2016/providence-college-mob-comes-anthony-esolen.

or religious orders. Thomas More is committed to the Roman Catholic tradition of liberal arts education, but its oversight comes entirely from laity in the church.

Similar dynamics obtained at Marquette University in a recent case over safe spaces and tolerance for diversity. Here it began with a student who may have been in violation of campus protections for minorities when he brought up bans on gay marriage in a philosophy class as an example that contradicted the Equal Liberty Principle. Later, outside class, the professor criticized the student for bringing up sensitive subjects that threatened campus policies designed to protect "safe" spaces. When another professor blogged about the incident, the university fired him. The reasons had to do with revealing the name of the professor who challenged the student and for violating the Guiding Values of Marquette, a Jesuit institution. The American Association of University Professors, an agency that protects the rights of faculty, has criticized the firing and opened an investigation. But again, writers for *Crisis Magazine* wondered, "Do faithful Catholics on Catholic campuses have the right to express their support for Catholic teachings on faith and morals?" At Marquette, "the answer seems to be no."[17]

Stories like these about Roman Catholic universities are by no means the exception and suggest that the differences between these institutions and mainline Protestant or formerly Protestant colleges and universities have become smaller and smaller. Indeed, the general tenor of Roman Catholicism since Vatican II has been to accommodate more and more to the secular trends of the wider society, at least in the United States. Of course Rome still forbids women's ordination and still teaches traditional sexual morality, though Pope Francis's recent encyclical on marriage and divorce has raised serious questions about the hierarchy's attachment to the older morality. Whether Vatican II is responsible for introducing these changes into the church is

---

17. Anne Hendershott, "Protecting Students from Catholicism at Marquette," *Crisis Magazine*, February 16, 2015, http://www.crisismagazine.com/2015/keeping -students-safe-catholic-teachings-marquette-university.

a matter of interpretation, though the council's goal of opening up the church to the modern world would seem to explain what is happening at Roman Catholic universities. But for Protestants to convert to Rome with the assumption that this is the church that Jesus founded and that this is a church that has not changed since the apostles is to be blind to the real conditions in the Roman Catholic Church. Some Roman Catholics applaud and some bemoan the current condition of the church. What is undeniable is that Roman Catholicism is no longer conservative. According to Richard A. Spinello, who uses Francis's encyclical on marriage to take the temperature of the church:

> The moral certitude implicit in Sacred Scripture is being dissolved in favor of a more relaxed paradigm where virtually every moral rule is subject to exception after a process of discernment.... The Catholic Church faces a dangerous cultural landscape in the years and decades ahead. It must contend with an unabated global Sexual Revolution that threatens marriage and family, and with ongoing threats to religious liberty. A divided and polarized Church cannot speak with a unified, convincing voice. But Pope Francis's mindset, which so effortlessly tolerates contradictions and polarities, mirrors the post-modern mentality that celebrates disunity and indeterminacy over unity, continuity, and moral closure. Thus, instead of the consistent clarity of mind and coherence of popes like Pius XI, Paul VI, and John Paul II, we encounter a web of incongruities and obscurities.[18]

Americanism Is Not the Problem—Modernism Is

For almost four centuries after the Reformation, the Roman Catholic Church was arguably the most conservative moral and social institution in the West. It was the source of the most opposition and the best critiques of the excesses of democracy, free markets, and scientific investigation. Not all Roman Catholics believed the hierarchy's opposition to change was smart or welcome. But the Vatican recognized many of the alterations that characterized liberal and secular soci-

---

18. Spinello, "*Amoris Laetitia* and the Post-Modern Papacy of Pope Francis."

eties would threaten the order and authority of the church. That is why Pope Leo XIII condemned Americanism as a heresy. The effort to adapt the church to a nation that separated church and state and protected religious diversity was ill equipped to preserve the ecclesiastical structures on which Roman Catholicism relied.

Rome's conservatism finally ran out of steam in the decades after the Second World War, and the rulings of the Second Vatican Council were indicative of a sense among the bishops that the church needed to take a different attitude to the surrounding society. Most scholars and journalists who study or write about the church know that the post–Vatican II church is substantially different from the one that stood against modernity for the better part of four centuries. The 2011 collection of essays in *The Crisis of Authority in Catholic Modernity* was indicative of the realization that Rome no longer had the authority—or was willing to act like it did—that had once characterized the pre–Vatican II church. In his introduction to the book, Michael J. Lacey observes the schizophrenic character of the contemporary Vatican. On the one hand, the papacy has a reach into the ordinary affairs of dioceses and parishes that is unprecedented in history. Much of this papal authority is owed to the advances of technology and communications that make the dissemination of the hierarchy's decisions much more direct than at any time in church history. On the other hand, the papacy's authority is more fragile and disputed than it ever has been. "When tensions arise between the official voice of the church, expressed in the teachings of the magisterium," Lacey writes, "and the voice of the layperson's conscience, the trend is clearly against the voice of authority and in favor of 'thinking on one's own.'" That freedom of conscience was in fact the "core value of moral autonomy in liberal modernity, against which the church in its long antiliberal, antimodern phase so stoutly contended."

Indeed, "thinking for oneself," the sort of intellectual independence of which prejudiced Protestants thought Roman Catholics incapable, has now become the chief characteristic of modern Roman Catholicism. And it puts stress on all the sorts of hierarchies, order, and certainties that Protestants think they acquire when they convert.

Thinking for oneself is at odds with "all the inherited conventions of traditional relations between the hierarchy and laity, the ordained and the merely baptized, the teaching church and the learning church."[19] Lacey concludes:

> For good or ill, this shift has gradually become characteristic of life within the church since Vatican II, and those who feel the need, as Cardinal Newman put it long ago, to toast conscience first and then the pope, are unapologetic. Prior to the council, such people might have drifted away from the faith and been encouraged from above to do so. Today, they feel their claims to belonging, reservations and all, are rightful and simply cannot be trumped by simply appealing to formal authority or citing those passages in scripture that buttress the idea of divinely instituted apostolic succession and its claim to exclusive spiritual powers of discernment. The children of the church have come haphazardly to feel like grown-ups and don't believe they have to abandon the family estate over differences in the family.[20]

The liberalism, freedom, and disorder that characterize Roman Catholicism since Vatican II means that when Protestants convert they are going to find a church with even more diversity than evangelicalism and almost the same amount of theological chaos and liturgical experimentation as in mainline Protestantism. While the modernism of the Roman Catholic Church is no reason to remain Protestant, Rome is not the answer to Protestantism's splintered state. If believing the articles of the Nicene Creed are important to being Christian, Protestantism's denominationalism has done a better job of preserving the teaching of the apostles than the bishops who claim to be the apostles' successors.

One measure is polling data. Only 63 percent of Roman Catholics and 66 percent of mainline Protestants believe in God, compared to 88 percent of evangelical Protestants and 89 percent of black

---

19. Michael J. Lacey, "Prologue: The Problem of Authority and Its Limits," in Michael J. Lacey and Francis Oakley, eds., *The Crisis of Authority in Catholic Modernity* (New York: Oxford University Press, 2011), 3.

20. Lacey, "Prologue: The Problem of Authority," 4.

Protestants. Questions about hell show similar results: 63 percent of Roman Catholics and 60 percent of mainline Protestants believe in hell compared to 82 percent of evangelicals (82 percent of black Protestants). And when it comes to same-sex marriage, 57 percent of Roman Catholics and 57 percent of mainline Protestants strongly favor gay marriage compared to 28 percent of evangelicals and 40 percent of black Protestants.[21]

Switching to Roman Catholicism is not the solution to the problems posed to Christianity by modern society.

---

21. Pew Research Center, "Religious Landscape Study," http://www.pewforum.org/religious-landscape-study/#religions.

CONCLUSION:
HOW TO BECOME A SAINT

A person who trusts Christ alone as Savior and has genuinely repented of her sins is a saint, according to Protestant teaching. The Second Helvetic Confession (1566), for instance, describes all such church members as saints: "The Church is an assembly of the faithful called or gathered out of the world; a communion, I say, of *all saints*, namely, of those who truly know and rightly worship and serve the true God in Christ the Savior, by the Word and Holy Spirit, and who by faith are partakers of all benefits which are freely offered through Christ" (ch. 17). Likewise, the Heidelberg Catechism places no distinction among Christians when it comes to the "communion of the saints." Any person who believes in Christ alone for salvation partakes "of him, and of all his riches and gifts" and must be ready to use his gifts and talents for "the advantage and salvation of other members" (A. 55). The Westminster Confession also describes a saint as anyone whom God "effectually calls" and who perseveres to the end. And despite the sins that still cling to believers, the sanctifying work of the Spirit continues so that "saints grow in grace, perfecting holiness in the fear of God" (ch. 13.3).

Indeed, by describing any true Christian as a saint, Protestants follow the language that the apostles used when addressing the early church. In Acts 9:32, Luke records that Peter addressed the "saints" at Lydda. Paul repeatedly addressed his epistles to the "saints" living in Rome or Corinth or Ephesus. An indication of how inclusive sainthood was for the apostles comes in Ephesians 3:8 where Paul considered himself to be among the "least of all the saints," even though God called him as an apostle to proclaim the gospel. The clear impression among Protestants and the New Testament is that saint-hood is not something reserved for a special class of Christians. It is the status of any person whom God has regenerated to believe the gospel and who belongs to the church.

That is a different way of understanding sainthood from the teaching and practice of the Roman Catholic Church. In his book on Roman Catholic sainthood, *Making Saints*, the veteran religion journalist Kenneth Woodward began his chapter on the history of sainthood with this concession: "Initially, the New Testament Chris-tians regarded all baptized believers as 'saints.'"[1] The rest of his book shows how far Roman Catholicism departed from that bibli-cal conception. Woodward's aim was not to criticize Rome for their approach to sanctity. He was merely trying to explain a process that often mystified church members as much as outsiders. But his book was unintentionally a vindication of the Reformation because Wood-ward showed how much the making of saints relied on the Vatican or on popularity and had little to do with the work of Christ.

The making of saints, like so much of Roman Catholic history, is a process that has changed over time and defies the apologists' reassurances of changelessness, stability, and rock-solid truth. The original saints prior to the fall of Rome in the fifth century were martyrs, monks, or heroic Christians who excelled in the faith and gained a quasi-divine status. Stephen, whose death Luke recorded in Acts 6, was the model for Christian martyrs—or witnesses to Christ. Monasticism arose as a way of imitating Christ without dying but still involving steadfast rejection of the world. When an exemplary Christian died, the living gathered around the deceased's tomb to be present with his or her remains. At this point, relics began to emerge as objects of divine presence, and the saints' burial places became destinations for pilgrimages. The historian of antiquity Peter Brown observes that by the sixth century Christianity was known more for

---

    1. Kenneth Woodward, *Making Saints: How the Catholic Church Determines Who Becomes a Saint, Who Doesn't, and Why* (New York: Simon and Schuster, 1996), 52.

its shrines and relics than for its worship of God. In fact, some of the earliest church leaders warned about worshiping saints and so tried to distinguish *latria* (worship) from *doulia* (veneration).Woodward rightly notes that this distinction, "though plausible in the abstract, was often difficult to maintain in practice."[2] The challenge of regulating the worship of saints was all the more difficult because the saints were creations of popular devotion, and bishops and popes always had trouble trying to regulate the people's piety. Sainthood, for much of the first thousand years of the church, was more a reflection of Roman Catholic populism than it was a set of procedures handed down from the magisterium. The reason was that people often believed that with a local saint the local parish had "their own heavenly patron." Sometimes the church's bishops did not even bother to resist popular sentiment. In 767 the Council of Nicaea decreed that every church altar, where the priest celebrated the Mass, needed to have an "altar stone" that housed a relic.[3]

By the tenth century, as the papacy was emerging as the supreme authority in the Western church, bishops and popes began to regulate sainthood. After all, the people could be wrong. What if they prayed to heretics, a problem that Augustine himself faced when Donatists who were avid for martyrdom were deemed heretical? The response was to require witnesses and evidence to demonstrate the sanctity of those deceased who would qualify. In fact, Pope Alexander III in 1170 decreed that no one could be venerated locally without papal authorization. This initiated a process that included witnesses who could testify to a saint's heroic performance of virtue and verify the miracles that Christians believed a saint had aided. By the fourteenth century, the papacy had established precise guidelines for sainthood that contributed further to the pope's power. This was the time when a papal determination of a saint became "infallible."[4] The new procedures did not, however, cut down on the number of saints the people

---

2. Woodward, *Making Saints*, 58.
3. Woodward, *Making Saints*, 60, 59.
4. Woodward, *Making Saints*, 68.

continued to pray to and venerate. This chaotic situation prompted the hierarchy to distinguish saints from the blessed, or the canonized (papally approved) from the beatified (the object of local veneration). But this distinction created yet another wrinkle—namely, that the saints approved by the church hierarchy were not popular with the people. The bishops wanted saints who excelled in virtue; the people wanted saints known for miraculous achievements. Either way, a saint was so far beyond the ordinary Christian that he or she produced a "treasury of merits" from which average believers could draw (while in purgatory) to qualify for heaven.

This system of sainthood, which percolated up from the parishes and which bishops tried to harness to maintain order, was precisely what prompted the Protestant Reformation. Europe was a society "drenched in saints," with feasts to honor them, pilgrimages to their shrines, and books—Woodward says they were "fully the equivalent of the modern romance"—that recounted their lives, and statues and images to celebrate their accomplishments.[5] Indeed, Protestant worship destroyed and denied the cult of the saints. Calvin especially replaced the altar with the pulpit, as words took over for images and the eye gave way to the ear. Luther, who had prayed to St. Anne for protection during a thunderstorm that prompted him to become a monk, eventually taught that a saint had no more sanctity than any other Christian. The reason was that all people who trusted Christ as their Savior received His righteousness as their own personal sanctity, imputed by faith alone. But Rome rejected the Protestant critique of sainthood. The Council of Trent reaffirmed the cult of saints and their relics, even though the bishops also pruned the list of saints to make room for later additions. Trent did manage to take over the entire process of canonization, a move that made possible Pope Benedict XIV's 1734 book on the beatification of saints to set the standard for modern Roman Catholicism. Eventually, the Vatican established an office that put potential saints through the paces to determine "scientifically" the authenticity of miracles and to document a life of holiness.

---

5. Woodward, *Making Saints*, 74.

Pope John Paul II made another adjustment in 1983 that attempted to simplify the process and place it more in the hands of local bishops than with the Vatican. Woodward describes the change as one that went from the courtroom with prosecutors and devil's advocate to an academic model in which a saint's supporters produced the equivalent of a doctoral dissertation that documented a life of sanctity. All the while, Rome's system had no warrant from the apostles' writings or experience. Roman Catholic canonization was not the sainthood that Jesus founded.

As fascinating as Woodward finds the history and process of saint-making and despite his Roman Catholic faith, he also acknowledges the problems and potential for abuse. For instance, in the case of Katherine Drexel (1858–1955), the foundress of the Sisters of the Blessed Sacrament for Indians and Colored People who gave away vast holdings from her Philadelphia family's fortune to the church, questions surrounding her views about race prompt Woodward to wonder about heroic virtue. Because Drexel refused to accept black candidates to her congregation, Woodward asks whether Drexel's advocates can simply say she was a product of her time. On the one hand, "it seems unfair to judge Mother Drexel…by the moral standards of later age." On the other hand, "saints are expected to meet standards beyond the norms for the rest of humankind." And if the point of creating a saint is to establish a model for other believers, in this case, to show that through Drexel the Roman Catholic Church in the United States "worked heroically for the true liberation…of Indians and blacks," then her failings on racial inclusion become a problem.[6] Aside from the question of whether Christians can ever rely on their own holiness, Woodward highlights the political and public relations calculations that sometimes influence the Vatican's decisions about sainthood. At a certain point, this process starts to look like what sports writers go through when voting on baseball players for the hall of fame.

---

6. Woodward, *Making Saints*, 233, 234.

A similar set of questions haunts the beatification of Pope John XXIII, who called the Second Vatican Council. Here the case of making a pope a saint was virtually unprecedented; the church had canonized only two popes since the Reformation. Even more astounding was an effort by liberal bishops and cardinals to make John a saint by public acclamation. Indeed, John's cause of sainthood was simply one more indication of the divisions at Vatican II between conservatives and progressives. The former opposed both the council and the pope responsible for calling it. Progressives took the opposite side. Woodward concedes that the "motives for acclaiming John's sainthood were as political as they were pious."[7] The way out of the dilemma was Pope Paul VI's determination to start the canonization process for both John XXIII and the pope conservatives favored—Pius XII. Rather than overcoming the divisions at the council, Pope Paul merely gave each side a cause by which to promote its concerns and thereby keep alive debates from the council.

Woodward includes several pragmatic concerns that reveal a tension between the theory of sainthood and the demands of Christian piety. On one level, the church may be guilty of creating too many saints. "It appears," he writes, "the church is burdened with an anomaly: a system which, for all its fastidiousness, is beatifying more people—many of them virtually indistinguishable in their stories and exemplarity from each other—than the faithful seem to want or need."[8] In other words, the system is supposed to produce models of piety and virtue for believers to emulate—a hierarchy of sanctity as it were. But with so many saints, Roman Catholics have trouble focusing on one and so neglect an alleged aid in the Christian walk. Another weakness is timeliness. A particularly holy person may have great appeal at a specific time, but the process of beatification and canonization takes so long that by the time he or she becomes a saint, the people to be inspired may be deceased. Woodward even wonders about the virtues used by church officials to evaluate potential saints.

---

7. Woodward, *Making Saints*, 283.
8. Woodward, *Making Saints*, 379.

The Vatican uses the classical (and pagan) virtues—prudence, justice, fortitude, and temperance—along with the Christian virtues of faith, charity, and hope to evaluate candidates. But, Woodward asks, "why not stress other virtues such as humility, patience, and mercy, which were emphasized by Jesus himself and are therefore qualities one might reasonably expect to find in a Christian saint? For that matter, why not look to the Beatitudes ('Blessed are the meek,' and so on) which Jesus recommended to his followers? In sum, why not stress Gospel values alone when analyzing the life of a saint?"[9] Whether Woodward knew it or not, he was asking precisely the questions that Protestant Reformers did when they began to compare the teaching of the apostles (Scripture) to the practices and teachings of the Roman Catholic Church. But once you do that, the whole edifice begins to shake.

In fact, the entire process and theology of making saints prove two essential points that this book has tried to establish: first, that the church the first Protestants faced was corrupt and leading souls astray, thereby not doing what Christ founded the church to do; second, that Roman Catholicism, despite tinkering here and there, is still in need of reformation. Indeed, Rome's canonization of "exemplary" Christians still demonstrates that the instincts of the Reformers on Scripture, salvation, worship, and church authority were sound and that all the errors they confronted still afflict Roman Catholicism.

Woodward himself admits that the New Testament, despite recording the martyrdom of Stephen in Acts 6, provides little warrant for the system of beatification and canonization that developed in Roman Catholicism. Stephen may have died for his faith, but in their epistles Paul and Peter referred to all Christians as saints. One good reason for that attitude was the centrality of faith in Christ. If people trusted Christ for forgiveness and repented of their sins, they were saints, especially by virtue of Christ's righteousness imputed to them by faith. No better form of sanctity could a person have than to

---

9. Woodward, *Making Saints*, 394.

approach God clothed in the spotless robe of Christ's sinlessness and complete obedience to the demands of God's law.

The Reformers—especially Luther—certainly questioned the profiteering that attended the making of saints. The notion that people could contribute to the church and in return receive merits from the treasury accumulated by saints that would reduce their time in purgatory was part of the abuse that drove Luther to raise his initial concerns about Rome. But the Reformers were concerned about more than ecclesiastical corruption. They also challenged a system that inferred, as the making of saints did, that some believers were holier than others by virtue of their heroism or their capacity to go beyond the normal lives of believers and achieve true sanctity. Rome may have talked about such virtue as the fruit of grace. Still, the idea that some Christians were truly holy and others were not, and that saints had extra merits from which the pope could draw to apply to other sinners and so lessen the time of purgation promoted the idea that what made someone a better Christian was works, not faith in Christ, and especially the works of other holy Christians, not the faithfulness of the only begotten Son of God. And the more the church acknowledged popular piety by anointing some Christians as worthy of sainthood, the more it cultivated devotion that looked not to Christ and His perfect life, death, and resurrection but to the holy lives of saints who could plead to God on others' behalf. As Woodward puts it, Luther "felt that a saint had no more grace than any other Christian." And since "Christians are justified by faith alone, he argued, they could not be saved through their own merits, much less those received through prayer from the 'treasury' of the saints."[10]

The Reformation did not simply curb corruption that sprang from abuses or propose a different understanding of sainthood with the doctrine of justification; Protestantism also sought a reform of worship. Again, the reason had much to do with the system of sainthood as developed by Rome. Churches were filled with relics,

---

10. Woodward, *Making Saints*, 75.

images, and statues of saints. Christians prayed to saints. Rather than ordinary believers approaching God through Christ alone, saints represented them before God. To be sure, Rome sometimes distinguished worship from veneration to ensure that Christians worshiped only God. Even so, the practice for ordinary church members, not to mention most priests and bishops, involved attributing superhuman or supernatural powers to those Christians who qualified as saints. Roman Catholics may not have worshiped a saint the way they worshiped God. But the veneration of extraordinary Christians, or saints, wound up doing precisely that to which the Reformers objected—veneration of saints distracted from the sufficiency of Christ. The proof of miracles aided by a saint encouraged Roman Catholics to look at those canonized as divine-like, thereby obscuring the uniqueness of Christ. Why appeal to a saint when you could pray directly to the Priest who sits at God's right hand, the only begotten Son of God Himself? The Reformation made a slogan not simply out of faith alone or grace alone. The Reformers also preached Christ alone precisely because Rome had allowed the gospel of Christ's saving work to become cluttered by the superhuman efforts of those the church deemed to be sufficiently holy to qualify as saints. When you throw into the equation the idea that saints are responsible in some way for miraculous occurrences, one of the requirements for sainthood, you can readily imagine that saints are closer to Jesus than to mere mortals. They may not be divine outright. Nevertheless, the system of sainthood facilitates a view of saints as divine-like. Purging worship of the trappings of sainthood and proclaiming Christ alone, then, was part and parcel of the Reformers' objections to the church's abuse of the system and the flawed theology that let sainthood continue to define Roman Catholic piety.

In the end, the fundamental divide between Rome and Protestantism remains what it was five centuries ago. Is Christ alone sufficient? Protestants insist that He is. Rome equivocates. Woodward quotes a statement from Roman Catholic theologians about saints, which asserts, "The Catholic tradition holds that Jesus Christ alone is never merely alone. He is always found in the company of a whole range of his friends, both living and dead."[11] Depending on how you understand "company," Protestants can affirm this and then extend the assertion to the entire body of Christ the way Paul did when he addressed the church in Corinth as saints. What about Scripture? Is the Bible sufficient to understand the gospel and worship? Protestants say yes. But again, Roman Catholics equivocate. Woodward concludes his book by writing that the "story of a saint is always a love story." This story reveals a "God who loves, and of the beloved who learns how to reciprocate and share that 'harsh and dreadful' love."[12] In other words, for Woodward the story of saints adds to the narrative of salvation revealed in Scripture. Once again Rome distracts from Christ and from what God has revealed in Scripture as sufficient for spiritual life and health with saints and their veneration. God revealed Himself in His Word and saved His people through the work of His Son, Jesus Christ. Rome added to what God did by including saints who supposedly show more grace and supplement what Christ accomplished according to the Bible. The Reformation pruned back Rome's supplementation of God's revealed will and Christ's life, death, and resurrection. When the Reformers asked Rome and then argued to cut back the growth of ecclesiastical bric-a-brac that had obscured the centrality of Scripture and the cross to salvation and the Christian life, the church's hierarchy condemned Protestantism's proposed reform.

That way of looking at the Reformation may be too tidy for some people. But given how the system of sainthood has continued to be such an important part of Roman Catholic devotion, that depiction of Protestantism captures the main features of the debates that split the Western church during the sixteenth century. Because Rome continues to elevate some Christians as heroic in their sanctity and still nurtures veneration of saints, it is still in need of reformation. And because Rome's system of sainthood continues to undermine

---

11. Woodward, *Making Saints*, 402.
12. Woodward, *Making Saints*, 406.

the centrality of Scripture, the sufficiency of Christ, and theocentric worship, reformation is still the burden for Roman Catholicism. It is not simply about abuses of sainthood or about venal popes or even sexual scandals. The gospel conveyed by Rome in the way it creates or acknowledges (depending on your perspective) saints is one that takes away from the sufficiency of Christ as revealed in Scripture. The gospel, truthfulness of Scripture, and danger of idolatry are still as much at stake in Roman Catholicism as they were at the time of the Reformation.

Protestants who contemplate "converting" to Rome need to understand the seriousness of the difference between their own faith and the one presented by Roman Catholicism. They may think they are joining with a form of Christianity that is more united, older, and so much more expansive and beautiful than the one in which their parents reared them. But they need to understand that if they join the Roman Catholic Church, they go from being saints to something else. If they join Rome, after death they will at best go to purgatory, unless of course they lead a life of extraordinary virtue that qualifies as saint-like. If they join Rome, they will need to draw from the treasury of merits in order to spend less time in purgatory, assuming they do not die in a state of mortal sin.

In other words, you cannot have the sufficiency of Christ that Protestantism teaches, the complete and entire righteousness that allows you to stand blameless on judgment day in God's presence— you cannot have that kind of sanctity and then add to it the alleged beauty, majesty, and holiness of Roman Catholicism. In the sixteenth century, you were either one or the other. You either trusted in Christ alone or you prayed to a saint who, along with Christ, might help you avoid sin and so spend less time in purgatory. That choice is still the issue today, five hundred years after Luther first objected to the corruptions, idolatry, and abuses that had grown up around the beatification and canonization of saints. If Luther was right about the Bible, believers go straight to heaven when they die. If Rome was right about the saints, a church member needs a lot of help, both from the living and the dead, to make it to heaven. On the upside,

Rome presents a lot of saints who may provide the needed assistance. On the downside, the hierarchy may be wrong about those saints. It would not be the first time that bishops and cardinals erred about the things of God.

INDEX